Top Rated™ Western Adventures

Top Rated Western Adventures

Top Rated™ Western Adventures

Guest Ranches, Pack Trips & Cattle Drives in North America

Edited by
Maurizio Valerio

THE DERRYDALE PRESS
Lanham and New York

THE DERRYDALE PRESS

Published in the United States of America
by The Derrydale Press
4720 Boston Way, Lanham, Maryland 20706

Distributed by NATIONAL BOOK NETWORK, INC.

First Derrydale printing with french folds, 2000

Artwork by Steamroller Studios; Cover art by Fifth Street Design; Maps by Map Art, Cartesia Software; Cartoons by Tom Novak, Novak Studio; Cover vertical photo and thumbnail by Nine Quarter Circle Ranch, Kim and Kelly Kelsey, Gallatin Gateway, Montana.

ISBN: 1-58667-006-9 (paperback : alk. paper)
Library of Congress Card Number: 00-102294

™ The paper used in this publication meets the minimum requirements of American National Standard for Information Sciences—Permanence of Paper for Printed Library Materials, ANSI/NISO Z39.48–1992. Manufactured in the United States of America.

To Allison, Marco and Nini

Top Rated Western Adventures

Table of Contents

Top Rated™ Western Adventures

Acknowledgments

It is customary in this section to give credit to those who have contributed to the realization of the end product. The Top Rated™ Guides started three years ago as a little personal crusade and has evolved into a totally challenging, stimulating and rewarding full time commitment.

My deep thanks must go first to all the Captains, Ranchers, Guides, Lodges and Outfitters who decided to trust our honesty and integrity. They have taken a leap of faith in sharing their lists of clients with us and for this we are truly honored and thankful.

They have constantly encouraged our idea. Captains have taught us the difference between skinny fishing and skinny dipping, while River Guides have patiently helped us to identify rafters, purlins, catarafts and J-rig rafts. They were also ready to give us a badly needed push forward every time this very time-consuming idea came to a stall. We have come to know many of them through pleasant phone chats, e-mails, faxes and letters. They now sound like old friends on the phone and we are certain we all share a deep respect for the mountains, the deserts and the waters of this great country of ours.

The Top Rated Team (both in the office and abroad), with months of hard work, skills, ingenuity, good sense of humor and pride, have then transformed a simple good idea into something a bit more tangible and much more exciting. They all have put their hearts in the concept and their hands and feet in the dirt. Some with a full-time schedule, some with a part-time collaboration, all of them bring their unique and invaluable style and contribution.

My true thanks to Brent Beck, Lindsay Benson, Robert Evans, Cheryl Fisher, Brian Florence, Jerry Hesseltine, Grace Martin, Kevin McNamara, Jerry Meek, Allison C. Mickens, Tom Novak, Slim Olsen, Shelby Sherrod, Giuseppe Verdi and Mr. Peet's Coffee and Tea.

Last, but not least, my sincere, profound, and loving gratitude to my wife Allison. Her patient support, her understanding, her help and her skills have been the fuel which started and stoked this fire. Her laughter has been the wind to fan it.

To you, Allison, with a toast to the next project...just kidding!

Maurizio Valerio

Preface

The value of information depends on its usefulness. Simply put, whatever allows you to make informed choices will be to your advantage. To that end, Top Rated™ Guides aims to take the guesswork out of selecting services for outdoor activities. Did you get what you paid for? From Top Rated™ Guides' point of view, the most reliable indicator is customer satisfaction.

The information in this book is as reliable as those who chose to participate. In the process of selecting the top professionals, Top Rated™ Guides contacted all licensed guides, outfitters and businesses which provide services for outdoor activities. They sought to include everyone but not all who were contacted agreed to participate according to the rules. Thus, the omission of a guide, outfitter or service does not automatically mean they didn't qualify based on customer dissatisfaction.

The market abounds with guidebooks by 'experts' who rate a wide range of services based on their personal preferences. The value of the Top Rated concept is that businesses earn a place in these books only when they receive favorable ratings from a majority of clients. If ninety percent of the customers agree that their purchase of services met or exceeded their expectations, then it's realistic to assume that you will also be satisfied when you purchase services from the outdoor professionals and businesses included in this book.

It's a fact of life; not everyone is satisfied all of the time or by the same thing. Individual experiences are highly subjective and are quite often based on expectations. One person's favorable response to a situation might provoke the opposite reaction in another. A novice might be open to any experience without any preconceived notions while a veteran will be disappointed when anything less than great expectations aren't met.

If you select any of the businesses in this book, chances are excellent that you will know what you are buying. A diversity of clients endorsed them because they believed the services they received met or exceeded their expectations. Top Rated™ Guides regards that information as more valuable than a single observer or expert's point of view.

The intent behind Top Rated™ Guides is to protect the consumer from being misled or deceived. It is obvious that these clients were given accurate information which resulted in a positive experience and a top rating. The number of questionnaire responses which included detailed and sometimes lengthy comments impressed upon us the degree to which people value their experiences. Many regard them as "once-in-a-lifetime" and "priceless," and they heaped generous praise on those whose services made it possible.

Top Rated™ Guides has quantified the value of customer satisfaction and created a greater awareness of top-rated outdoor professionals. It remains up to you to choose and be the judge of your own experience. With the help of this book, you will have the advantage of being better informed when making that pick.

Robert Evans, *information specialist*

The Top Rated™ Concept

Mission Statement

The intent of this publication is to provide the outdoor enthusiast and his/her family with an objective and easy-to-read reference source that would list only those businesses and outdoor professionals who have **agreed to be rated** and have been overwhelmingly endorsed by their past clients.

There are many great outdoor professionals (Guides, Captains, Ranches, Lodges, Outfitters) who deserve full recognition for putting their experience, knowledge, long hours, and big hearts, into this difficult job. With this book we want to reward those deserving professionals while providing an invaluable tool to the general public.

Top Rated™ Guides are the only consumer guides to outdoor activities.

In this respect it would be useful to share the philosophy of our Company, succinctly illustrated by our Mission Statement:

> "To encourage and promote the highest professional and ethical standards among those individuals, Companies, Groups or Organizations who provide services to the Outdoor Community.
>
> To communicate and share the findings and values of our research and

surveys to the public and other key groups.

To preserve everyone's individual right of a respectful, knowledgeable and diversified use of our Outdoor Resources."

Our business niche is well defined and our job is simply to listen carefully.

THEY "the Experts" versus WE "the People"

Top Rated books were researched and compiled by **asking people such as yourself**, who rafted, fished, hunted or rode a horse on a pack trip with a particular outdoor professional or business, to rate their services, knowledge, skills and performance.

Only the ones who received A- to A+ scores from their clients are found listed in these pages.

The market is flooded with various publications written by 'experts' claiming to be the ultimate source of information for your vacation. We read books with titles such as The Greatest River Guides, The Complete Guide to the Greatest Fishing Lodges, etc.

We do not claim to be experts in any given field, but we rather pass to history as good....listeners. In the preparation of the Questionnaires we listened first to the outdoor professionals' point of view and then to the comments and opinions of thousands of outdoor enthusiasts. We then organized the findings of our research and surveys in this and other publications of this series.

Thus we will not attempt to tell you how to fish, how to paddle or what to bring on your trip. We are leaving this to the outdoor professionals featured in this book, for they have proven to be outstanding in providing much valuable information before, during and after your trip.

True [paid] advertising: an oxymoron

Chili with beans is considered a redundant statement for the overwhelming majority of cooks but it is an insulting oxymoron for any native Texan.

In the same way, while 'true paid advertising' is a correct statement for some, it is a clear contradiction in terms for us and certainly many of you. A classic oxymoron.

This is why we do not accept commissions, donations, invitations, or, as many publishers cleverly express it, "...extra fees to help defray the cost of publication". Many articles are written every month in numerous specialized magazines in which the authors tour the country from lodge to lodge and camp to camp sponsored, invited, or otherwise compensated in many different shapes or forms.

It is indeed a form of direct advertising and, although this type of writing usually conveys a good amount of general information, in most cases it lacks the impartiality so valuable when it comes time to make the final selection for your vacation or outdoor adventure.

Without belittling the invaluable job of the professional writers and their integrity, we decided to approach the task of **researching information and sharing it with the public** with a different angle and from an opposite direction.

Money? ... No thanks!

We are firmly **committed to preserve the impartiality** and the novelty of the Top Rated idea.

For this reason we want to reassure the reader that the outdoor professionals and businesses featured in this book have not paid (nor will they pay), any remuneration to Top Rated™ Guides or the editor in the form of money, invitations or any other considerations.

They have earned a valued page in this book solely as the result of ***their hard work and dedication to their clients.***

"A spot in this book cannot be purchased: it must be earned"

Size of a business is not a function of its performance

Since the embryonic stage of the Top Rated idea, during the compilation of the first Top Rated book, we faced a puzzling dilemma.

Should we establish a minimum number of clients under which a business or outdoor professional will not be allowed to participate in our evaluating process?

This would be a 'safe' decision when it comes the time to elaborate the responses of the questionnaires. But we quickly learned that many outdoor professionals limit, by choice, the total number of clients and, by philosophy of life, contain and control the size of their business. They do not want to grow too big and sacrifice the personal touches or the freshness of their services. In their words "we don't want to take the chance to get burned out by people." They do not consider their activity just a job, but rather a way of living.

"WHY, NO MAM, WE NEVER HAVE HAD ANY OF THOSE SASQUATCH SIGHTINGS IN THESE PARTS."

But if this approach greatly limits the number of clients accepted every year we must say that these outdoor professionals are the ones who often receive outstanding ratings and truly touching comments from their past clients.

Some businesses have provided us with a list of clients of 40,000, some with 25 . In this book **you will find both the large and the small.**

From a statistical point, it is obvious that a fly fishing guide who submitted a list of 32 clients, by virtue of the sample size of the individuals surveyed, will implicitly have a lower level of accuracy if compared to a business for which we surveyed 300 guests. (Please refer to the Rating and Data Elaboration Sections for details on how we established the rules for qualification and thus operated our selection).

We do not believe that the size of business is a function of its good performance and we feel strongly that those dedicated professionals who choose to remain small deserve an equal chance to be included.

We tip our hats

We want to recognize all the Guides, Captains, Ranches, Lodges and Outfitters who have participated in our endeavor, whether they qualified or not. The fact alone that they accepted to be rated by their past clients is a clear indication of how much they care, and how willing they are to make changes.

We also want to credit all those outdoor enthusiasts who have taken the time to complete the questionnaires and share their memories and impressions with us and thus with you. Some of the comments sent to us were hilarious, some were truly touching.

We were immensely pleased by the reaction of the outdoor community at large. The idea of "Top Rated™ Guides" was supported from the beginning by serious professionals and outdoor enthusiasts alike. We listened to their suggestions, their comments, their criticisms and we are now happy to share this information with you.

Questionnaires

"Our books will be only as good as the questions we ask."

We posted this phrase in the office as a reminder of the importance of the 'tool' of this trade. The questions.

Specific Questionnaires were tailored to each one of the different activities surveyed for this series of books. While a few of the general questions remained the same throughout, many were specific to particular activities. The final objective of the questionnaire was to probe the many different facets of that diversified field known as the outdoors.

The first important factor we had to consider in the preparation of the Questionnaires was the total number of questions to be asked. Research shows an *inversely proportionate relation* between the total number of questions and the percentage of responses: the higher the number of questions, the lower the level of response. Thus we had to balance an acceptable return rate with a meaningful significance. We settled for a compromise and we decided to keep 20 as the maximum number.

The first and the final versions of the Questionnaires on which we based our surveys turned out to be very different. We asked all the businesses and outdoor professionals we contacted for suggestions and criticisms. They helped us a great deal: we weighed their different points of view and we incorporated all their suggestions into the final versions.

We initially considered using a phone survey, but we quickly agreed with the businesses and outdoor professional that we all are already bothered by too many solicitation calls when we are trying to have a quiet dinner at home. We do not want you to add Top Rated to the list of companies that you do not want to talk to, nor do we want you to add our 800 number to your caller ID black list.

In using the mail we knew that we were going to have a slightly lower percentage of questionnaires answered, but this method is, in our opinion, a more respectful one.

We also encouraged the public to participate in the designing of the questionnaire by posting on our website at www.topratedsurveys.com the opportunity to submit a question and ...."Win a book". Many sent their suggestions and , if they were chosen to be used in one of our questionnaires, they were given the book of their choice.

Please send us your question and/or your suggestions for our future surveys to:

Top Rated™ Surveys, P.O. Box 718, Baker City, OR 97814

Rating (there is more than one way to skin the cat)

We considered many different ways to score the questionnaires, keeping in mind at all times our task:

translate an opinion into a numerical value

Some of the approaches considered were simple *averages* [arithmetical means], others were sophisticated statistical tests. In the end we opted for simplicity, sacrificing to the God of statistical significance. WARNING: if $p \leq 0.001$ has any meaning in your life stop reading right here: you will be disappointed with the rest.

For the rest of us, we also made extensive use in our computation of the *median*, a statistic of location, which divides the frequency distribution of a set of data into two halves. A quick example, with our imaginary Happy Goose Outfitter, will illustrate how in many instances the *median* value, being the center observation, helps in describing the distribution, which is the truly weak point of the *average*:

Average salary at Happy Goose Outfitters $ 21,571

Median salary at Happy Goose Outfitters $ 11,000

5,000	10,000	10,000	11,000	12,000	15,000	98,000
Wrangler	Guide	Guide	Senior Guide	Asst.Cook	Cook	Boss

Do not ask the boss : “What’s the average salary?”

These are the values assigned to **Questions 1-15**:

5.00 points	OUTSTANDING
4.75 points	EXCELLENT
4.25 points	GOOD
3.50 points	ACCEPTABLE
3.00 points	POOR
0.00 points	UNACCEPTABLE

Question 16, relating to the weather conditions, was treated as bonus points to be added to the final score.

Good=0 Fair=1 Poor=2

The intention here was to reward the outdoor professional who had to work in adverse weather conditions.

Questions 17 - 18 = 5 points

Questions 19 - 20 = 10 points

The individual scores of each Questionnaire were expressed as a percentage to avoid the total score from being drastically affected by one question left unanswered or marked “not applicable.” All the scores received for each individual outdoor professional and business were thus added and computed.

The 90 points were considered our cutoff point. Note how the outfitters must receive a combination of Excellent with only a few Good marks (or better) in order to qualify.

Only the Outfitters, Captains, Lodges, Guides who received an A- to A+ score did qualify and they are featured in this book.

We also decided not to report in the book pages the final scores with which the businesses and the outdoor professionals ultimately qualified. In a way we thought that this could be distractive.

In the end, we must admit, it was tough to leave out some outfitters who scored very close to the cutoff mark.

It would be presumptuous to think that our scoring system will please everybody, but we want to assure the reader that we tested different computations of the data. We feel the system that we have chosen respects the overall opinion of the guest/client and maintains a more than acceptable level of accuracy.

We know that .... "You can change without improving, but you cannot improve without changing."

The Power of Graphs (how to lie by telling the scientific truth)

The following examples illustrate the sensational (and unethical) way with which the 'scientific' computation of data can be distorted to suit one's needs or goals.

The *Herald* presents a feature article on the drastic increase of total tonnage of honey stolen by bears (mostly Poohs) in a given area during 1997.

Total tonnage of honey stolen by bears (Poohs)

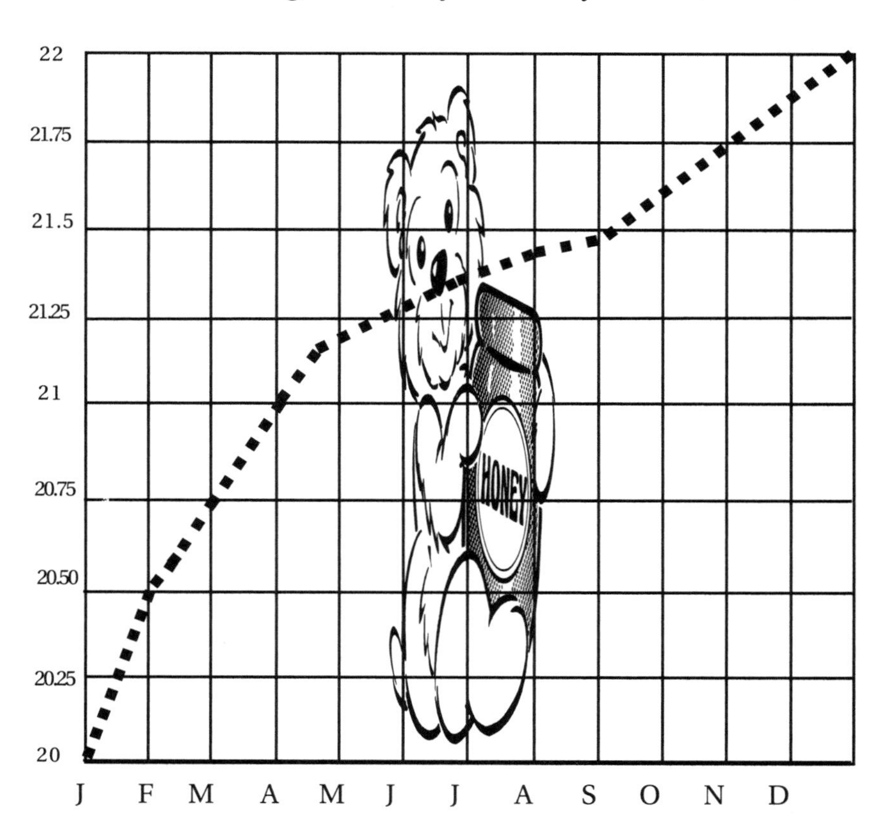

It is clear how a journalist, researcher or author must ultimately choose one type of graph. But the question here is whether or not he/she is trying to make "his/her point" by choosing one type versus the other, rather than simply communicate some findings.

Please note that the bears, in our example, are shameless, and remain such in both instances, for they truly love honey!

Graphs were not used in this book. We were just too worried we wouldn't use the correct ones.

The Book Making Process

Research

We **researched** the name and address of every business and outdoor professional **in the United States and** in all the **provinces of Canada** (see list in the Appendix). Some states do not require guides and outfitters or businesses providing outdoor services to be registered, and in these instances the information must be obtained from many different sources [Outfitter's Associations, Marine Fisheries, Dept. of Tourism, Dept. of Environmental Conservation, Dept. of Natural Resources, Dept. of Fish and Game, US Coast Guard, Chamber of Commerce, etc.].

In the end the database on which we based this series of Top Rated™ Guides amounted to more than 23,000 names of Outfitters, Guides, Ranches, Captains etc. Our research continues and this number is increasing every day. The Appendix in the back of this book is only a partial list and refers specifically to Top Rated Western Adventures.

Participation

We **invited** businesses and outdoor professionals, with a letter and a brochure explaining the Top Rated concept, to join our endeavor by simply sending us a **complete list of their clients** of the past two years. With the "Confidentiality Statement" we reassured them that the list was going to be kept **absolutely confidential** and to be *used one time only* for the specific purpose of evaluating their operation. Then it would be destroyed.

We truly oppose this "black market" of names so abused by the mail marketing business. If you are ever contacted by Top Rated you may rest assured that your name, referred to us by your outdoor professional, will never be sold, traded or otherwise used a second time by us for marketing purposes.

Questionnaires

We then **sent a questionnaire** to **every single client on each list** (to a maximum of 300 randomly picked for those who submitted large lists with priority given to overnight or multiple day trips), asking them to rate the

services, the **knowledge** and **performance** of the business or outdoor professional by completing our comprehensive questionnaire (see pages 192-193). The businesses and outdoor professionals found in these pages may or may not be the ones who invest large sums of money to advertise in magazines, or to participate at the annual conventions of different clubs and foundations. However, they are clearly the ones, according to our survey, that put customer satisfaction and true dedication to their clients first and foremost.

Data Elaboration

A **numerical value was assigned to each question**. All the **scores were computed**. Both the **average** and the **median** were calculated and considered for eligibility. Please note that the total score was computed as a percentile value.

This allows some flexibility where one question was left unanswered or was answered with a N/A. Furthermore, we decided not to consider the high and the low score to ensure a more evenly distributed representation and to reduce the influence which an extreme judgement could have either way (especially with the small sample sizes).

We also set a **minimum number of questionnaires** which needed to be answered to allow a business or an outdoor professional to qualify. Such number was set as a function of the total number of clients in the list: the smaller the list of clients, the higher was the percentage of responses needed for qualification.

In some cases the outfitter's average score came within 1 point of the A-cutoff mark. In these instances, we considered both the median and the average were considered as well as the guests' comments and the total number of times that this particular business was recommended by the clients by answering with a 'yes' question 19 and 20.

Sharing the results

Top Rated will share the results of this survey with the businesses and the outdoor professionals. This will be done at no cost to them whether or not they qualified for publication. All questionnaires received will, in fact, be returned along with a summary result to the business, keeping the confidentiality of the client's name when this was requested. This will prove an invaluable tool to help improving those areas that have received some criticisms.

The intention of this series of books is to research the opinions and the comments of outdoor enthusiasts, and to share the results of our research with the public and other key groups.

One outfitter wrote us about our Top Rated™ Guides series, "I feel your idea is an exciting and unique concept. Hopefully our past clientele will rate us with enough points to 'earn' a spot in your publication. If not, could we please get a copy of our points/questionnaires to see where we need to improve. Sincerely..."

This outfitter failed to qualify by just a few points, but such willingness to improve leaves us no doubt that his/her name will be one of those featured in our second edition. In the end it was not easy to exclude some of them from publication, but we are certain that, with the feedback provided by this survey, they will be able to improve those areas that need extra attention.

We made a real effort to keep a position of absolute impartiality in this process and, in this respect, we would like to repeat that the outfitters have not paid, nor they will pay, one single penny to Top Rated™ Guides or the Editor to be included in this book.

The research continues.

Top Rated
Icon Legend

General Services and Accommodations

General Services and Accommodations

General Services

Season(s) of operation

Activities

HORSEBACK

LLAMA PACK TRIPS

HORSE PACK TRIPS

BARREL RACING

ROPING

TEAM PENNING

TEAM ROPING

STEER WRESTLING

WAGON RIDES

GHOST TOWN TOURS

BRANDING

CUTTING

CATTLE DRIVES

Activities/Fishing Techniques

Activities

SUPERVISED SPORTS

RACQUETBALL COURT

TENNIS COURT

SWIMMING

WHITEWATER TRIPS

MUZZLELOADER

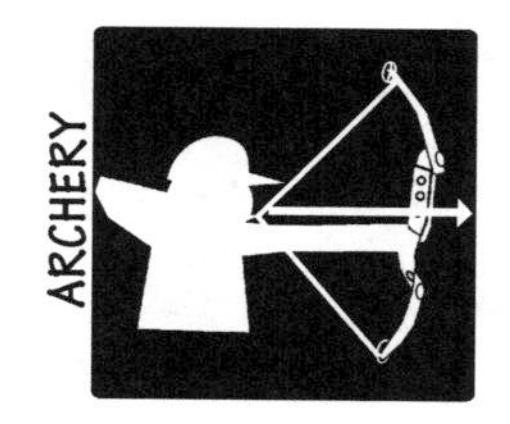
ARCHERY

TARGET SHOOTING

GOLFING

HIKING / TREKKING

ATV RIDING

CANOEING

SNOWMOBILE TOURS

Activities

BIRD WATCHING

WILDLIFE VIEWING

SNOWSHOEING

MOUNTAIN BIKING

HIKING/TREKKING

CROSS COUNTRY

DANCING

LIVE ENTERTAINMENT

WATERFOWL HUNTING

CLAY SHOOTING

BIG GAME HUNTING

BIRD HUNTING

Top Rated
Ranches, Outfitters and Pack Stiations

Top Rated Professionals in

Alaska

Outdoor Professionals

License and Report Requirements

- State requires licensing of Outdoor Professionals.
- State requires a "Hunt Record" for big game.
- Saltwater Charter Vessels Logbook Program - Charter Vessel guided trips are required to submit pages of logbook on a weekly basis.
- Charter Vessels are required to be licensed with the Commercial Fisheries Entry Commission at Juneau, phone: (907) 789-6150

Useful information for the state of

Alaska

State and Federal Agencies

Alaska Dept. of Fish & Game
PO Box 25526
Juneau, AK 99802-5526
phone: (907) 465-4180 Fish
(907) 465-4190 Game

Alaska Region Forest Service
709West 9th Street
Box 21628
Juneau, AK 99802-1628
phone: (907) 586-8863
TTY: (907) 586-7816
www.fs.fed.us/r10

Chugach National Forest
3301 C Street, Ste. 300
Anchorage, AK 99503-3998
phone: (907) 271-2500
TTY: (907) 271-2332

Tongass National Forest:
Sitka Office
204 SiginakaWay
Sitka, AK 99835
phone: (907) 747-6671
TTY: (907) 747-4535
fax: (907) 747-4331

Tongas National Forest:
Federal Building
Ketchikan, AK 99901-6591
phone: (907) 228-6202
fax: (907) 228-6215

Bureau of Land Management
Alaska State Office
222W. 7th Avenue, #13
Anchorage, AK 99513-7599
phone: (907) 271-5960
or (907) 271-plus extension
fax: (907) 271-4596
http://www.ak.blm.gov

Office Hours: 8:00 a.m. - 3:45 p.m.

National Parks

Denali National Park & Preserve
phone: (907) 683-2294

Gates of the Arctic National Park
phone: (907) 456-0281

Glacier Bay National Park
phone: (907) 697-2230

Katmai National Park
phone: (907) 246-3305

Kenai Fjords National Park
phone: (907) 224-3175

KobukValley National Park
phone: (907) 442-3890

Lake Clark National Park
phone: (907) 271-3751

Wrangell-St. Elias National Park
phone: (907) 822-5234

Yukon-Charley Rivers National Park
phone: (907) 456-0593

Associations, Publications, etc.

Dude Ranches.com
http://www.duderanches.com

American Fisheries Society
2720 Set Net Ct.
Kenai, AK 99611
phone: (907) 260-2909
fax: (907) 262-7646

Trout Unlimited Alaska Council
PO Box 3055
Soldotna, AK 99669
phone: (907) 262-9494

Federation of Fly Fishers
http://www.fedflyfishers.org

Lost Creek Ranch

Les and Norma Cobb
P.O. Box 84334 • Fairbanks, AK 99708
phone: (907) 672-3999
email: alaskalcr@worldnet.att.net

Lost Creek Ranch is located 150 miles northwest of Fairbanks, Alaska.

Les Cobb has lived and hunted the area for 25 years.

Lost Creek Ranch uses horses, river boats, and ATVs. If you are looking for a horseback pack hunt or a Yukon or Tanana River hunt by boat, the ranch provides professional guides with more than 25 years each of hunting experience in Alaska. Lost Creek Ranch also supplies drop-off hunts by horse or boat.

Since it is a guest ranch, there is always something for the whole family to enjoy together, such as trail riding, fishing, nature hikes, or the pioneer flavor of life with peace and quiet all around.

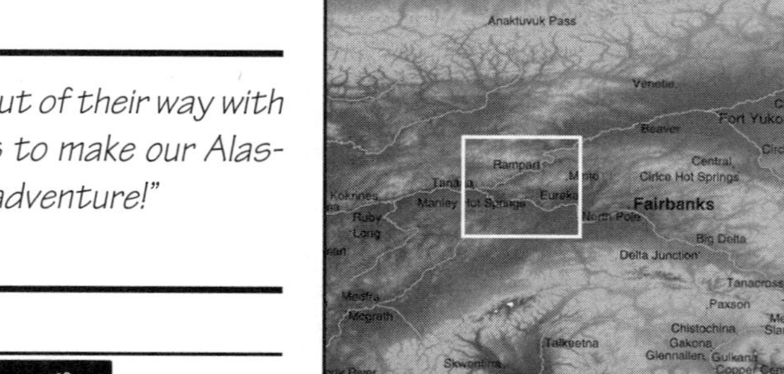

"Les & Norma went out of their way with us and other guests to make our Alaskan trip an Alaskan adventure!"
Peter Burokas

SEASONS OF OPERATION

WESTERN ACTIVITIES

ACTIVITIES

SERVICES

Lost Creek Ranch

Top Rated Professionals in
California

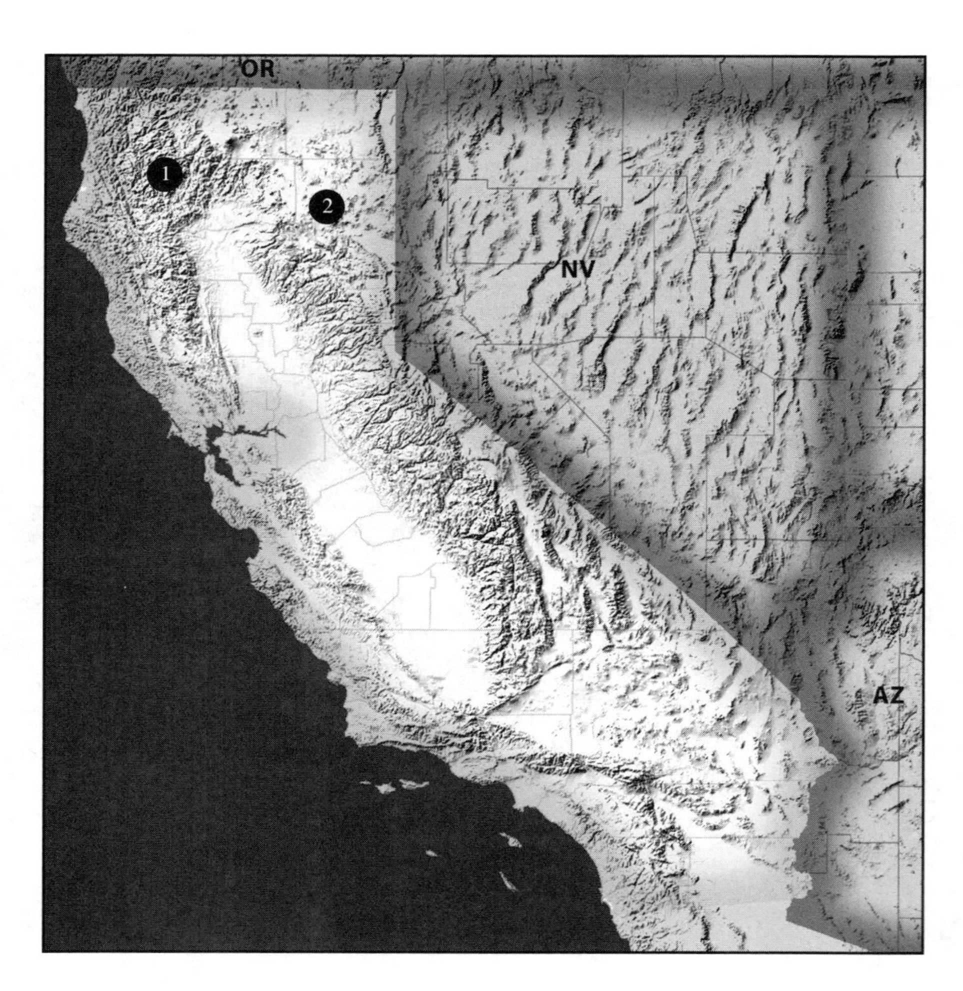

Outdoor Professionals

1. Coffee Creek Ranch
2. Spanish Springs Ranch

Useful information for the state of

California

State and Federal Agencies

California Fish & Game Commission
License & Revenue Branch
3211 "S" Street
Sacramento, CA 95816
phone: (916) 227-2245
fax: (916) 227-2261
http://www.dfg.ca.gov

Pacific Southwest
Forest Service Region
630 Sansome St.
San Francisco, CA 94111
phone: (415) 705-2874
TTY: (415) 705-1098

Bureau of Land Management
California State Office
2800 Cottage Way
Sacramento, CA 95825
fax: (916) 978-4657
http://www.ca.blm.gov

Office Hours: 8:30 - 4:30 pm (PST)

National Parks

Lassen Volcanic National Park
phone: (530) 595-4444

Redwood National Park
phone: (707) 464-6101

Sequoia & Kings Canyon Natl. Parks
phone: (209) 565-3341

Yosemite National Park
phone: (209) 372-0200

Channel Islands National Park
phone: (805) 658-5700

Associations, Publications, etc.

California Trout, Inc.
870 Market St. #859
San Francisco, CA 94102
phone: (415) 392-8887
http://www.caltrout.org

Trout Unlimited, California Chapter
1024 C. Los Gamos
San Rafael, CA 94903-2517
phone: (415) 472-5837
http://cwo.com/~trout/index.html

Federation of Fly Fishers
http://www.fedflyfishers.org

Bass Chapter Federation
751 Melva Ave.
Oakdale, CA 95361
phone: (209) 541-3673
or (209) 847-3272

California Outdoors
PO Box 401
Coloma, CA 95613
phone: (800) 552-3625
http://www.caloutdoor.org

License and Report Requirements

- State requires licensing of Outdoor Professionals.
- State requires the filing of a "Monthly Guide Log" for all outdoor professionals, including river outfitters.
- River Outfitters need a "Use Permit", required for BLM, National Forest, Indian reservations, and National Parks.
- Boat and Waterways Dept. requires license for all motorized craft, and raft or floating device if carrying more than 3 persons.

Coffee Creek Ranch

Ruth Hartman
HC 2, Box 4940 – Dept AW • Trinity Center, CA 96091
phone: (800) 624-4480 • fax: (916) 266-3597

Picture-postcard views await you with snowcapped mountains and sparkling lakes in the Trinity Alps Wilderness. Coffee Creek, an excellent fly fishing stream, runs wild through the 127 acres owned and operated by the Hartman Family. Secluded cabins, nutritious meals, pool and spa, hayrides, stocked fishpond, gold panning, nightly entertainment, hiking, supervised children's activities for 3 to 17 year-olds, and baby-sitting during rides for those under 3.Scenic mountain trails, some roping and horsemanship lessons, and gymkhana. Spring, fall and senior discounts. Romantic weekends. Fall foliage. Hunting for deer and bear and pack trips. Adult-only weeks. Wedding and reception packages, maximum 250 persons; small meetings-conferences, maximum 50.

Winter cross country skiing, horse-drawn sleigh rides. Pickup service available from Redding, free for Trinity Center airport (private planes).

"The cabin accommodations are set next to the creek, the sound was so relaxing. The people have a yesteryear's friendly spirit and 'aim to please' attitude. I recommend Coffee Creek to anyone searching for a vacation with western flavor"
Marilyn McIntosh

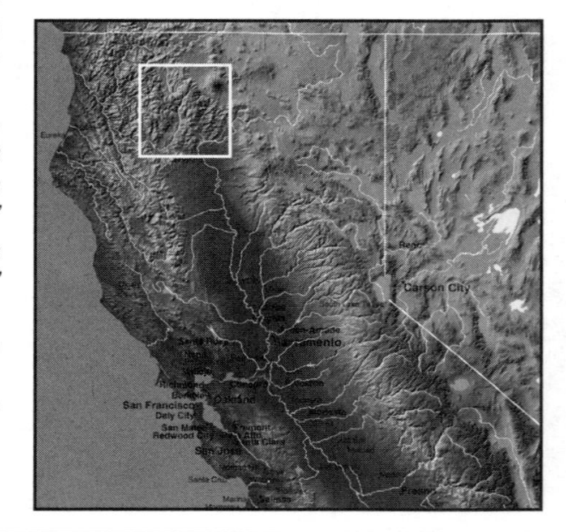

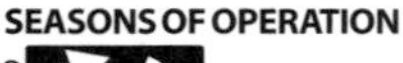

SEASONS OF OPERATION

WESTERN ACTIVITIES

ACTIVITIES

SERVICES

NH
NORTHERN CALIFORNIA'S
FINEST
GUEST RANCH
coffee
creek

Spanish Springs Ranch

Barbara Roberts
Highway 395 • Ravendale, CA 96123 • reservations: 801 A St. • San Rafael, CA 94901
phone: (800) 272-8282 • fax: (415) 456-4073
email: Spanishs@SpanishSprings.com • http://www.SpanishSprings.com

Spanish Springs Ranch provides guests with authentic Western vacations. Spanish Springs is a working cattle ranch. 70,000 pristine acres make for some of the most breathtaking horseback riding in the world. The ranch also features 4,000 cattle and more than 100 horses.

Activities include horseback riding, swimming, trap shooting, roping, tennis, hiking, and much more.

The ranch is open from April through October. We offer comfortable facilities with all the amenities, and three hearty meals a day. Our goal is to provide each guest with the most enjoyable vacation possible.

There are always many great events happening at Spanish Springs Ranch. As you know, any time is a great time to come up and enjoy the Ranch.

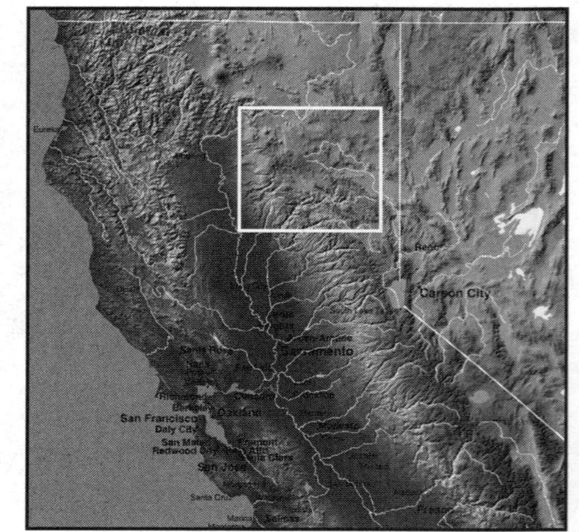

"Thorough knowledge of the region and attention to safety offer the right mix of excitement and relaxation. At the end of each day the chuck wagon is miraculously transformed into one of the finest open air cafes west of the Rockies!" Alex Estreicher

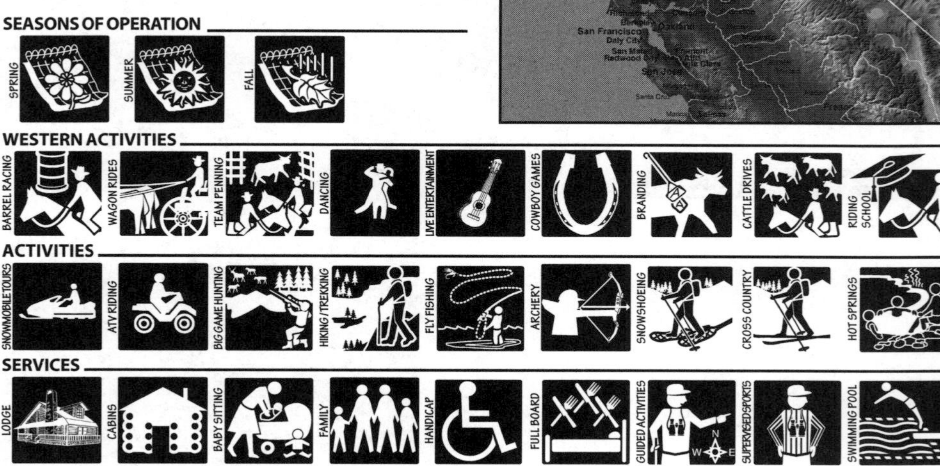

SPANISH SPRINGS
R·A·N·C·H
You Have Arrived
SPANISH SPRINGS

Top Rated Professionals in

Colorado

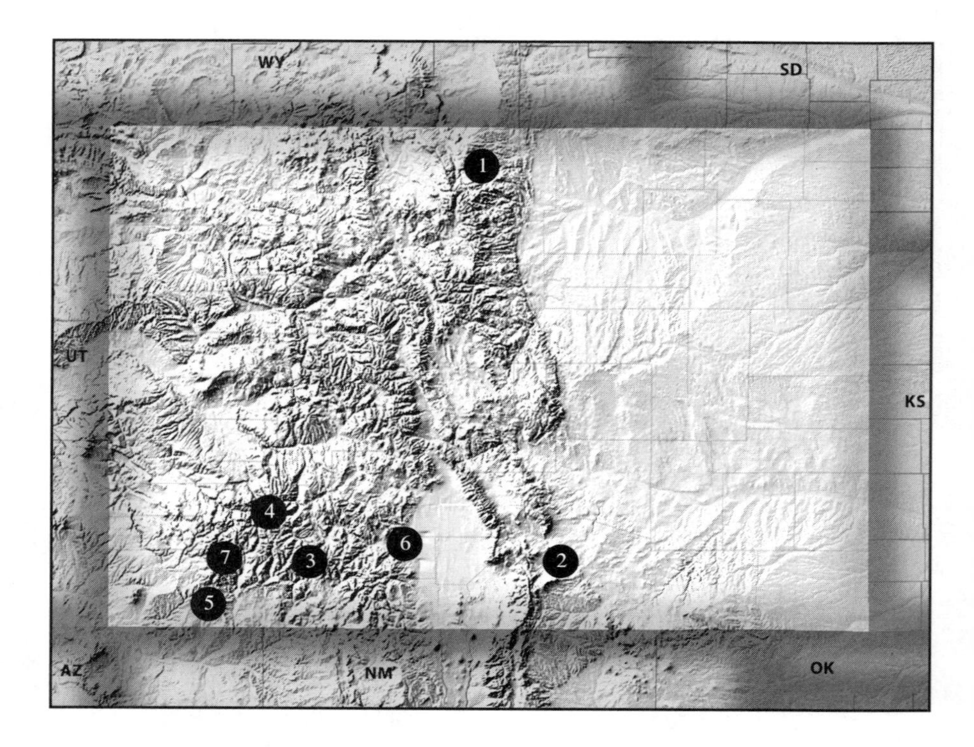

Outdoor Professionals

1. Beaver Meadows Resort Ranch
2. Echo Canyon Guest Ranch
3. Frazier Outfitting
4. Lakeview Resort & Outfitters
5. San Juan Outfitting
6. Schmittel Packing & Outfitting
7. Skyline Guest Ranch

License and Report Requirements

- State requires licensing of Outdoor Professionals.
- State requires an "Inter-Office Copy of Contract with Client" be submitted each time a client goes with an Outfitter. Colorado Agencies of Outfitters Registry sends this copy to client to fill out and return to their agency.
- Colorado State Forest Service requires a "Use Permit" for all guided activities on federal land.

Useful information for the state of

Colorado

State and Federal Agencies

Colorado Agencies of Outfitters Registry
1560 Broadway, Suite 1340
Denver, CO 80202
phone: (303) 894-7778

Colorado Dept. of Natural Resources
1313 Sherman, Room 718
Denver, CO 80203
phone: (303) 866-3311

Forest Service
Rocky Mountain Region
740 Simms Street
PO Box 25127
Lakewood, CO 80225
phone: (303) 275-5350
TTY: (303) 275-5367

Arapaho-Roosevelt National Forests
Pawnee National Grassland
phone: (970) 498-2770

Grand Mesa-Uncompahgre
Gunnison National Forests
phone: (970) 874-7641

Pike-San Isabel National Forests
Comanche & Cimarron National
Grasslands
phone: (719) 545-8737

San Juan-Rio Grande National Forest
phone: (719) 852-5941

White River National Forest
phone: (970) 945-2521

Bureau of Land Management
Colorado State Office
2850 Youngfield St.
Lakewood, Co. 80215-7093
phone: (303) 239-3600
fax: (303) 239-3933
Tdd: (303) 239-3635
Email: msowa@co.blm.gov
Office Hours: 7:45 a.m. - 4:15 p.m.

National Parks

Mesa Verde National Park, CO 81330
phone: (303) 529-4465

Rocky Mountain National Park
phone: (303) 586-2371

Associations, Publications, etc.

Colorado Dude & Guest Ranch Assoc.
PO Box 300
Tabernash, CO 80478
phone: (970) 887-3128
directory: (970) 887-9248
fax: (970) 887-2456

The Dude Ranchers' Association
PO Box F-471
LaPorte, CO 80535
phone: (970) 223-8440
fax: (970) 223-0201

The Dude & Guest Ranches of Grand
County
phone: (800) 247-2636
http://dude-ranch.com/body/html

DudeRanches.com
http://www.duderanches.com

Beaver Meadows Resort Ranch

Don and Linda Weixelman

100 Marmot Dr. #1 • PO Box 178 • Red Feather Lakes, CO 80545
phone: (800) 462-5870 • (970) 881-2450 • fax: (970) 881-2643
email: info@beavermeadows.com

Beaver Meadows is a full-service destination resort with a relaxed, family-oriented atmosphere in a breathtaking setting. Located on the North Fork of the Cache La Poudre River, our ranch occupies 320 acres of mountain meadows, willow creeks, lodgepole forests and quaking aspen groves.

Open year-round, we've provided group and vacation services for more than 20 years. Our staff is committed to providing individual attention and quality service to every event that we host.

We offer year-round activities. Our 22-mile trail system is used for extensive equine activities, mountain biking, hiking, cross-country skiing and showshoeing. Lessons and guides are available for all these activities. Activities are not included in our nightly rates unless a package is requested.

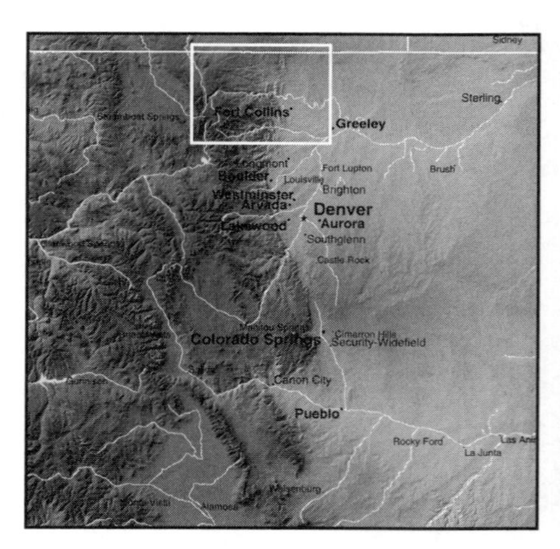

"Beaver Meadows provided outstanding service and were a joy to work with...and just being GREAT. Will definitely be back again and again!" Denise Noble

SEASONS OF OPERATION

WESTERN ACTIVITIES

ACTIVITIES

SERVICES

Beaver Meadows Resort Ranch

Echo Canyon Guest Ranch

Bob Kennemer

P.O. Box 328 • La Veta, CO 81055

phone: (800) 341-6603 • (719) 742-5524 • fax: (719) 742-5525

email: echo@rmi.net • www.guestecho.com • Lic. #1143

Echo Canyon affords its guests a "unique western adventure."

We're proud of our quality riding program for beginners as well as riders who can work cattle.

We match our riders with athletic horses that we own and train.

Your "unique western adventure" includes trail rides, roping lessons, cattle work, overnight pack trip, cookout, cowboy entertainment, trout ponds, shooting range, 4 x 4 tours, game area, hot tub, delicious food, quality rooms and cabins.

Our scenery is spectacular. We are located at 8,500 feet elevation beneath West Spanish Peak in Southern Colorado where wildlife abounds.

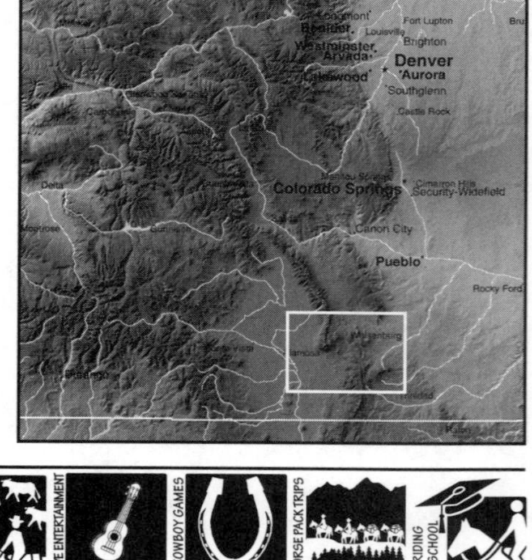

"This was truly the best vacation we ever had! This ranch was first class all the way." Renee Cruea

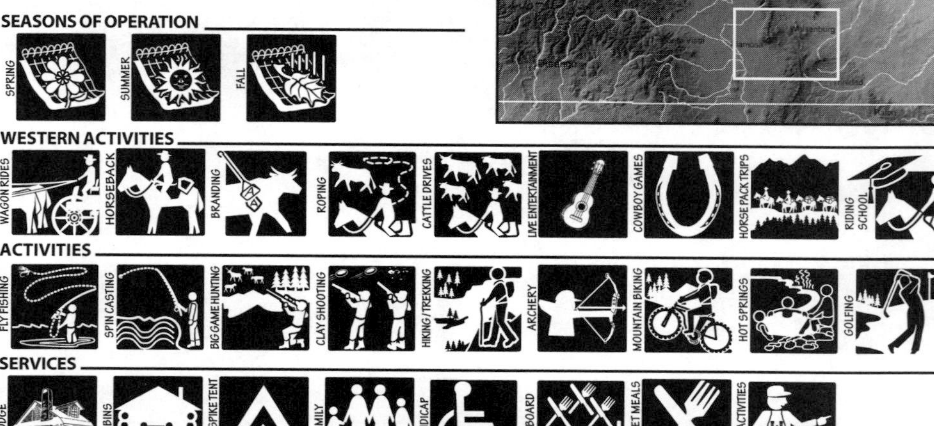

ECHO CANYON
Colorado
GUEST RANCH

Frazier Outfitting

Sammy Frazier
HC 34, Box 81 • Rye, CO 81069
phone: (719) 676-2964 • license #1738
email: coloradotrips@hotmail.com • www.sportsmandream.com

We are a horseback operation offering full service tent camps at an elevation of 11,300 feet. This includes the option of taking day rides from the base camps to 13,000 feet. The alpine terrain provides spectacular opportunities for photography, nature study, wildlife viewing, fishing and relaxing. Of particular interest are the small lakes and miles of high-country streams filled with trout, along with abundant herds of wild elk grazing the meadows and drainages. We also offer pack-in/out service for campers and backpackers.

Frazier Outfitting operates 40 miles southwest of Creede, Colorado, at the headwaters of the Rio Grande River and surrounded by the Continental Divide. Permitted access includes both the Rio Grande National Forest and the WeminucheWilderness.

This is a small business specializing in personal, quality, outdoor experience.

"Honesty, integrity and a burning desire to please clients are Sammy's attributes." Barry Iden

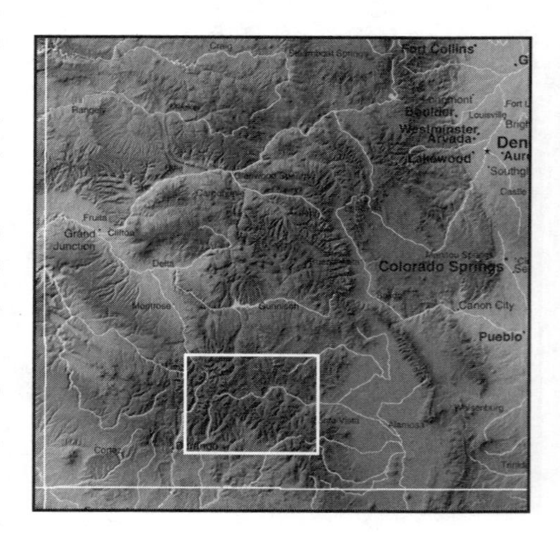

SEASONS OF OPERATION

WESTERN ACTIVITIES

ACTIVITIES

SERVICES

FRAZIER
OUTFITTING

Lakeview Resort and Outfitters

Dan and Michelle Murphy
Box 1000 • Lake City, CO 81235
*phone: (800) 456-0170 • (970) 944-2401 • fax: (970) 641-5952 * Lic. # 939*

The Lakeview Resort is located on the shores of Lake San Cristobal, in many folks' opinion, the most beautiful lake in Colorado.

We have lodge rooms, spacious suites and quaint cabins with woodburning fireplaces or stoves.

The Lakeview Resort offers a family atmosphere with many adventurous activities. We offer fishing boats, family pontoon boats and new Jeeps for rent. Expert guided fishing is available on the lake.

Exciting horseback activities are also available, with two-hour rides, sunset supper rides, all-day historic or fishing rides and overnight pack trips.

We have the most complete conference center facility in the Lake City area.

"I cannot praise them enough. They went above and beyond the call of duty to make my experience a treasured memory."

SEASONS OF OPERATION

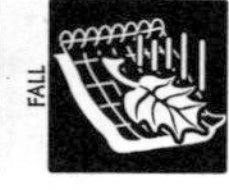

WESTERN ACTIVITIES

ACTIVITIES

SERVICES

GUIDED ACTIVITIES

LAKEVIEW
RESORT, INC
& OUTFITTERS, INC.

San Juan Outfitting

Tom and Cheri Van Soelen
186 County Rd. 228 • Durango, CO 81301
phone: (970) 259-6259 • fax: (970) 259-2652
email: sjo@frontier.net • www.subee.com/sjo/ • Lic. # 997

San Juan Outfitting specializes in classic western horse pack trips. We offer only high-quality trips catering to small groups.

Our spring pack trips take you into the ruins of the ancients (Anasazi Indians) for three to four days.

Summer and fall pack trips for fishing, photography and relaxing takes you into the heart of the Weminuche Wilderness to a base camp just below the Continental Divide at an elevation of 10,300 feet.

Our high country lake trip travels portions of the Divide while fishing some of the high lakes.

The ultimate adventure is our Continental Divide ride. We travel approximately 100 miles of the Divide at an average elevation of 12,500 feet.

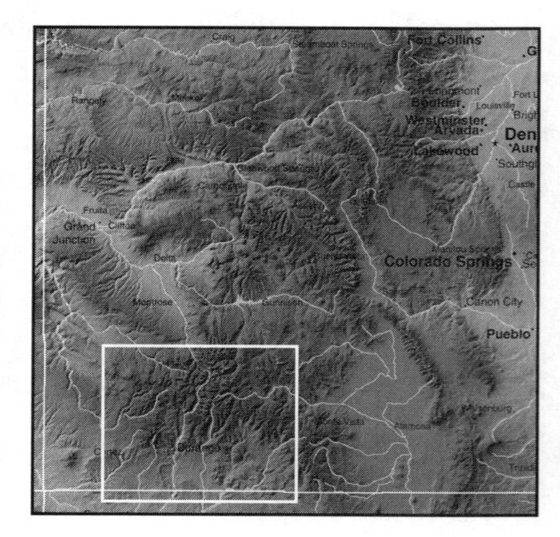

"The whole thing from food, to horses, to living quarters, to friendliness, to 'you name it' was perfect!" Spencer McLean

SEASONS OF OPERATION

WESTERN ACTIVITIES

ACTIVITIES

SERVICES

Schmittel Packing & Outfitting

David and Verna Schmittel
15206 Hwy. 285 • Saguache, CO 81149
phone: (719) 655-2722 • Lic. # 344

Schmittel Packing and Outfitting has provided exciting, high-quality pack trips for 30 years in the wilderness and non-wilderness areas of the San Juan/Rio Grande and Gunnison National Forests, located in "America's Switzerland" of southwestern Colorado.

The area provides a spectacular opportunity to enjoy excellent trail horses, abundant and varied wildlife, unique riding experiences and excellent meals. Dave and Verna have hosted guests with varied riding abilities from every state and many foreign countries.

No one has to be a seasoned rider to enjoy the gorgeous scenery and good company. Each trip is different, allowing guests to visit this magnificent region again and again. Member of Colorado Outfitters Association, Rio Grande Chapter of the Colorado Outfitters Association, and People for the West.

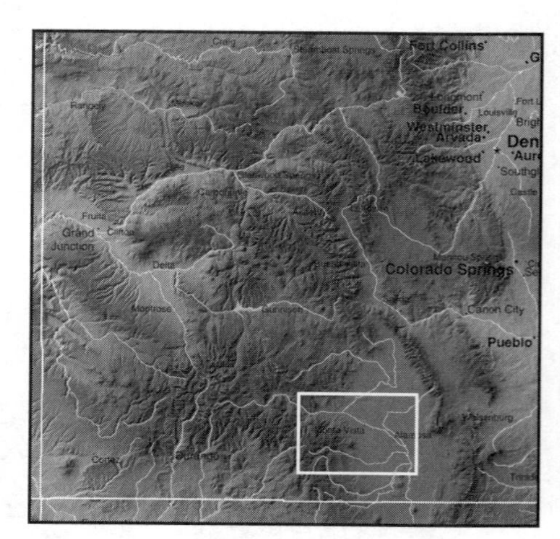

"It is a privilege and a pleasure to horsepack with Dave and Verna Schmittel, and the finest string of pack horses I have ever experienced."
Ronald F. Cox

SEASONS OF OPERATION

WESTERN ACTIVITIES

ACTIVITIES

SERVICES

SCHMITTEL PACKING & OUTFITTING

Skyline Guest Ranch

Sheila and Mike Farny
PO Box 67 • Telluride, CO 81435
phone: (888) 754-1126 • (970) 728-3757 • fax: (970) 728-6728
email: skyline-ranch@toski.com

A warm western welcome awaits you, your family and friends at Skyline Guest Ranch. We are committed to sharing with you a special spirit we call "Mountain Joy." Camaraderie flourishes, adventures are shared and there is time for special moments in surroundings of unsurpassed beauty and peace.

You may choose to spend your holiday in one of our ten lodge rooms, each with private bath, or in one of our housekeeping cabins which sleep from two to six people. Skyline is located three miles from the Telluride ski area where you will find some of the finest, uncrowded slopes in the West.

In winter, we offer sleigh rides, cross country skiing, and fine dining. In summer you will enjoy riding one of our horses, fishing in our three trout-filled lakes or riding a mountain bike to an abandoned ghost town.

"...the Farny's and Skyline staff are definitely a cut above their competition!"
Elaine & Doug Moore

SEASONS OF OPERATION

WESTERN ACTIVITIES

ACTIVITIES

SERVICES

SKYLINE
GUEST RANCH

Top Rated Professionals in
Idaho

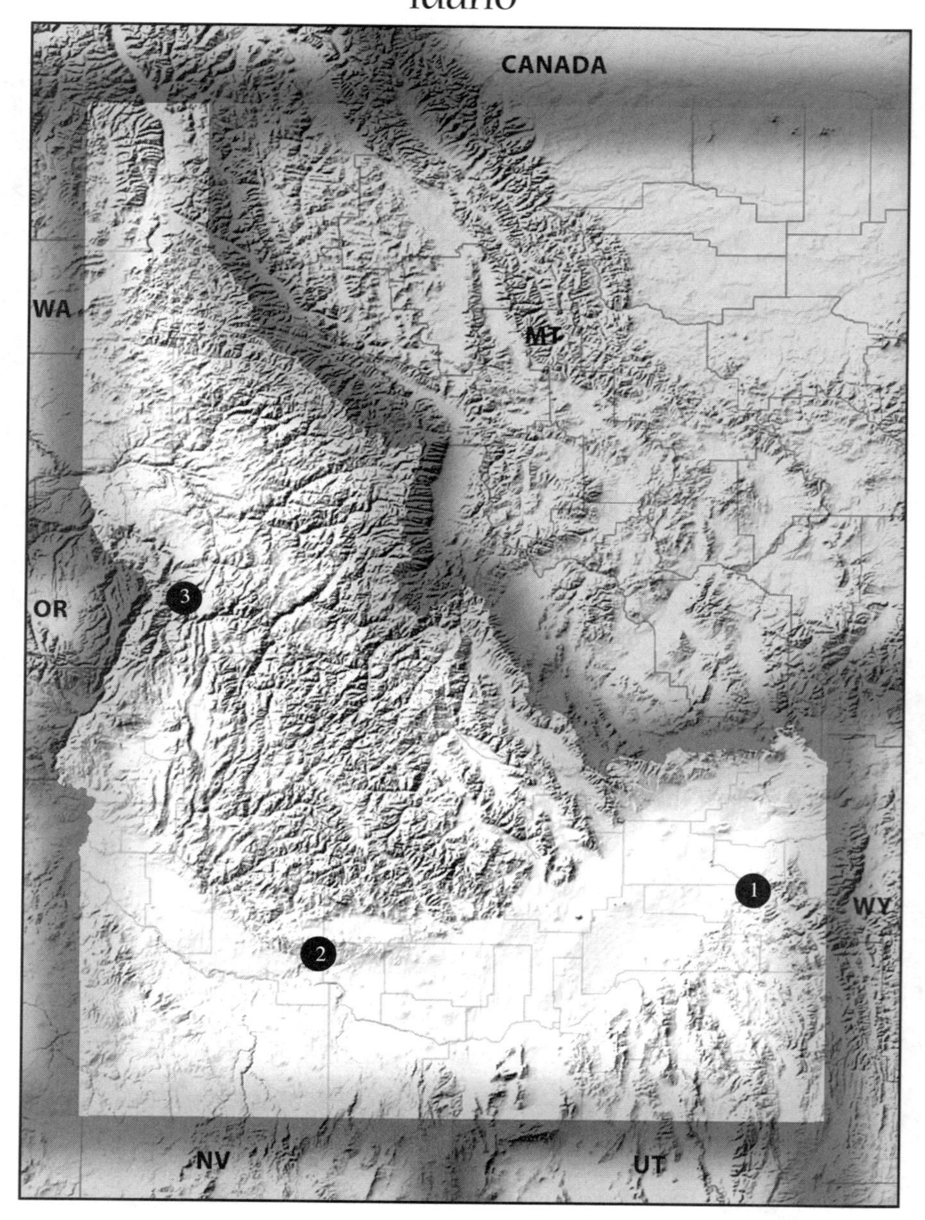

Outdoor Professionals

1. Granite Creek Guest Ranch
2. Venture Outdoors
3. Wind River Outfitters

Useful information for the state of

Idaho

State and Federal Agencies

Idaho Fish & Game Dept.
600 South Walnut
Boise, ID 83707
phone: (208) 334-3700
fax: (208) 334-2114

Outfitter & Guides Licensing Board
1365 N. Orchard, Room 172
Boise, ID 83706
phone: (208) 327-7380
fax: (208) 327-7382

Forest Service
Northern Region
Federal Bldg.
PO Box 7669
Missoula, MT 59807-7669
phone: (406) 329-3616
TTY: (406) 329-3510

Clearwater National Forest
phone: (208) 476-4541

Idaho Panhandle, Coeur d'Alene, Kaniksu, St. Joe National Forests
phone / TTY: (208) 765-7223

Nez Perce National Forest
phone: (208) 983-1950

Bureau of Land Management
Idaho State Office
1387 S. Vinnell Way
Boise, ID 83709-1657
phone: (208) 373-3896
or (208) 373-plus extension
fax: (208) 373-3899
Office Hours 7:45 a.m. - 4:15 p.m.

Associations, Publications, etc.

Idaho Outfitters & Guides Association
PO Box 95
Boise, ID 83701
phone: (208) 342-1438
fax: (208) 338-7830
Email: info@ioga.org • http://www.ioga.org

Idaho Guest and Dude Ranch Assoc.
HC 72
Cascade, ID 83611
phone: (208) 382-4336
message phone: (208) 382-3217

DudeRanches.com
http://www.duderanches.com

Trout Unlimited Idaho Council
212 N. Fourth Street #145
Sandpoint, ID 83864-9466
phone: (208) 263-4433
fax: (208) 265-2996

American Fisheries Society
Edward D. Koch
3765 La Mesita Way
Boise, ID 83072
phone: (208) 378-5293
Email: ted_koch@mail.fws.gov

Federation of Fly Fishers
http://www.fedflyfishers.org

Idaho Bass Chapter Federation
President: Allan Chandler
9906 W. Deep Canyon Drive
Star, ID 83669
phone: (208) 859-5433 (day)
Email: chandlr@micron.net

License and Report Requirements

- State requires licensing of Outdoor Professionals.
- State requires that every Outfitter be it bird, fish, big game, river rafting, trail riding or packing file a "Use Report" annually.
- Bureau of Land Management requires Special Use Permit for commercial guiding on BLM property.
- Currently, no requirements for Guest/Dude Ranches.

Granite Creek Guest Ranch

Carl and Nessie Zitlau

P.O. Box 340 • Ririe, ID 83443
phone: (208) 538-7140 • fax: (208) 538-7876
email: granite@srv.net • www.srv.net/~granite

Granite Creek Guest Ranch is one of the most scenic cattle ranches in the West.

Nestled against the border of Caribou National Forest, it is comprised of about 2,600 acres of mountainous timber and range land, and 400 acres of farm land.

The Zitlau family has raised cattle here since the early 1900s.

It is a "real" working cattle ranch with just the right touch of civilization. Families, couples and singles of all ages and horse skills have a terrific time.

Ranch activities include wonderful home-cooked meals, rustic cabins with private baths, fishing in the private lake, a variety of terrain for great trail riding, and our specialty — cattle drives and roundups.

"My 16-year-old son enjoyed this more than anything else we've ever done, and we've done a lot." Kathy Crowley

SEASONS OF OPERATION

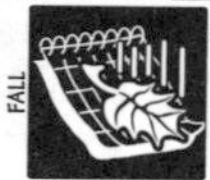

WESTERN ACTIVITIES

ACTIVITIES

SERVICES

GRANITE CREEK GUEST RANCH

Venture Outdoors

Dave Markham and Sue Barney

PO Box 2251 • Hailey, ID 83333

phone: (800) 528-LAMA (5262) • fax: (208) 788-5049

email: venout@micron.net • www.ventureoutdoorsidaho.com

Sun Valley, Idaho, is one of the most spectacular resorts in the West and it is located in the heart of one of America's most scenic alpine regions, surrounded by jagged peaks, clear mountain lakes and streams and renowned for its pristine natural beauty.

Imagine leading a gentle, well-trained llama to a beautiful campsite near a crystal clear lake, then imagine this intelligent and unusual pack animal is carrying your personal gear on his back. We provide trail head transport, informative, adventurous guides and superb international cuisine. Hike through spectacular scenery in the mountain ranges surrounding Sun Valley with a fun loving, naturalist guide. Travel the backcountry while your guide identifies Idaho's unique wildflowers, majestic peaks, and wildlife. Bike the backcountry roads and trails on guided day and multi-day trips. Whether a downhill cruise or a challenging single-track, our expert guides are always there to help with riding tips and to discuss the natural history of the area.

"The Llamas were a joy! We laughed the whole way! We would definitely do it again and have recommended it to friends."
Michelle Kuper-Smith

SEASONS OF OPERATION

WESTERN ACTIVITIES

ACTIVITIES

SERVICES

Wind River Outfitters

Michael and Jaylene Branson
5265 Highway 30 South • New Plymouth, ID 83221
phone: (800) 854-6697 • (208) 278-3706 • fax: (208) 278-3703
email: mike@windriveroutfitters.com • www.windriveroutfitters.com

Hunting, fishing, family vacation, trail rides, pack trips, backpacking and just good old fashion fun. Wind River Outfitters' camps are back country wilderness camps. Step back in time and enjoy the country just as the early travelers did. Stay in comfortable canvas cabins, furnished with wood stoves and cots with foam pads.

There are numerous trails to choose from for the novice to the more experienced rider. We are committed to good service at affordable prices.

We also offer big game hunting: elk, whitetail deer, mule deer, bear and mountain lion. We have many different packages to choose from.

Let us know what you would like in YOUR vacation and we will do what we can to provide it.

"The food & fellowship was excellent, the fishing exciting, the scenery beautiful. Time went much too fast!"
Ron & Genny Diekemper, Carlyle, IL

SEASONS OF OPERATION

WESTERN ACTIVITIES

ACTIVITIES

SERVICES

OVERNIGHT TRIPS

Top Rated Professionals in

Montana

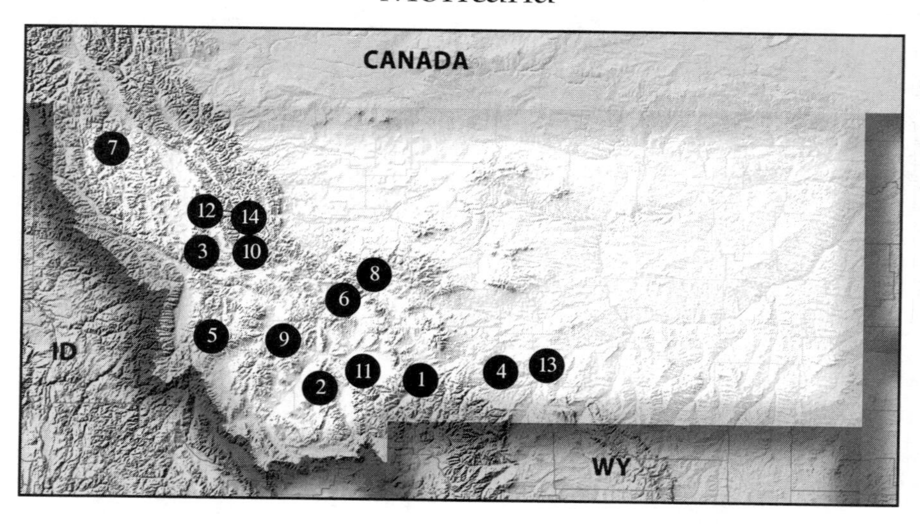

Outdoor Professionals

1. Beartooth Plateau Outfitters, Inc.
2. Broken Arrow Lodge
3. Cheff Guest Ranch
4. Double Spear Ranch
5. Esper's Under Wild Skies Lodge & Outfitters
6. EW Watson & Sons Outfitting
7. Hargrave Cattle & Guest Ranch
8. Hidden Hollow Hideaway
9. Iron Wheel Ranch
10. Monture Face Outfitters
11. Nine Quarter Circle Ranch
12. Rich Ranch, LLC
13. Three Cross Ranch
14. WTR Outfitters

License and Report Requirements

- State requires licensing of Outdoor Professionals.
- State requires an "Annual Client Report Log" for all Hunting and Fishing Outfitters.
- State does not regulate River Guides.
- Guest/Dude Ranches need to get an Outfitter license only if they take guest to fish or hunt on land that they do not own.

Useful information for the state of

Montana

State and Federal Agencies

Montana Board of Outfitters
Dept. of Commerce
Arcade Building - 111 North Jackson
Helena, MT 59620-0407
phone: (406) 444-3738

Montana Dept. of Fish, Wildlife & Parks
1420 East 6th
Helena, MT 59620
phone: (406) 444-2535

Forest Service
Northern Region
Federal Building
PO Box 7669
Missoula, MT 59807-7669
phone: (406) 329-3616
TTY: (406) 329-3510

Bitterroot National Forest
phone: (406) 363-3131

Custer National Forest
phone / TTY: (406) 248-9885

Flathead National Forest
phone: (406) 755-5401

Gallatin National Forest
phone / TTY: (406) 587-6920
fax: (406) 587-6758

Helena National Forest
phone: (406) 449-5201

Kootenai National Forest
phone: (406) 293-6211

Lewis & Clark National Forest
phone: (406) 791-7700

Lolo National Forest
phone: (406) 329-3750

Bureau of Land Management
Montana State Office
Granite Tower
222 North 32nd Street
P.O. Box 36800
Billings, Montana 59107-6800
phone: (406) 255-2885
fax: (406) 255-2762
Email - mtinfo@mt.blm.gov
Office Hours: 8:00 a.m. - 4:30 p.m.

National Parks

Glacier National Park
phone: (406) 888-5441

Associations, Publications, etc.

DudeRanches.com
http://www.duderanches.com

Fishing Outfitters Assoc. of Montana
PO Box 67
Gallatin Gateway, MT 59730
phone: (406) 763-5436

Federation of Fly Fishers
PO Box 1595
502 South 19th, Ste. #1
Bozeman, MT 59771
phone: (406) 585-7592
fax: (406) 585-7596
http://www.fedflyfishers.org

Trout Unlimited Montana Council
Council Chairman: Michael A. Bushly
2611 - 5th Avenue South
Great Falls, MT 59405-3023
phone: (406) 727-8787
fax: (406) 727-2402
Email: mbushly@cmrussell.org
http://www.montanatu.org

Montana Bass Chapter Federation
12345 O'Keefe Road
Missoula, MT 59812
phone: (406) 728-8842

Beartooth Plateau Outfitters, Inc.

Ronnie L. Wright
P.O. Box 1127 • Cooke City, MT 59020-1127
phone: (800) 253-8545 • (406) 838-2328 June-Sept. • (406) 445-2293 Oct.-May

I'd like to invite you to let us be your hosts and show you the Yellowstone Park backcountry and the Absaroka-Beartooth Wilderness high lake area.

We operate out of three pack stations located at: Cooke City, Roberts, and Wisdom, Montana. The Cooke city Pack Station is our headquarters for our summer and early fall season.

Our pack trips into the Absaroka-Beartooth Wilderness offer literally hundreds of high, pristine, alpine lakes full of a wide variety of trout (cutthroat, brook, golden and rainbow), and arctic grayling. Our Yellowstone Park pack trips offer secluded fishing in famous trout waters such as: the Lamar River and Slough Creek. Whether you go to the Absaroka-Beartooth Wilderness or into Yellowstone, the abundance of wildlife, beautiful wildflowers, waterfalls and towering granite peaks offer infinite photography, sight-seeing opportunities and just plain relaxin'. Orvis® Fly Fishing Expedition Outfitter.

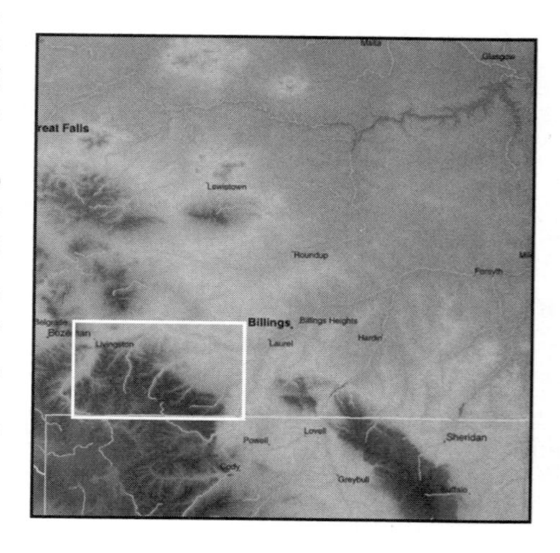

"My vacation exceeded all of my expectations! It honestly was the best trip I have ever taken. I would definitely do this trip again!" Jennifer Collins, Charleston, SC

SEASONS OF OPERATION

WESTERN ACTIVITIES

ACTIVITIES

SERVICES

BEARTOOTH PLATEAU OUTFITTERS

Broken Arrow Lodge

Erwin and Sherry Clark

2200 Upper Ruby Rd., Box 177 • Alder, MT 59710
phone: (800) 775-2928 • phone/fax: (406) 842-5437
www.recworld.com/state/mt/hunt/broken/broken.html

Broken Arrow Lodge is located in the Snowcrest Mountain Range in Southwest Montana's Ruby Valley. The Ruby River flows through the property and is only a moment's walk away.

Broken Arrow Lodge is a modern facility known for friendly, personalized service in a homey atmosphere. We supply lodging, meals (served at your convenience), and year-round recreation. Activities include fishing, hunting, family vacations, horseback riding, wildlife viewing, winter sports, lodge activities, and more.

Five rooms are available with space for one to four, or a family-size room with space for up to eight. Rooms are clean and comfortable with your choice of single or double beds. Large front deck provides a great area to relax and view the breathtaking scenery, abundant wildlife, and beautiful wildflowers.

Airport shuttle service is available as well as equipment rental, fax, and satellite TV.

"The hospitality was wonderful...we felt like we were visiting friends." Mary Ann McGuire

SEASONS OF OPERATION

WESTERN ACTIVITIES

ACTIVITIES

SERVICES

Broken Arrow Lodge
ULTIMATE OUTDOOR EXPERIENCE
MONTANA

Cheff Guest Ranch

Mick and Karen Cheff
4274 Eagle Pass Rd. • Charlo, MT 59824
phone: (406) 644-2557

A world of wondrous natural beauty and superb outdoor recreation awaits you at the Cheff Guest Ranch.

The working cattle and horse ranch lies on a mountainside overlooking the beautiful Mission Valley. Explore the beauty of our area on foot or horseback.

Flathead Lake, the National Bison Range, and Glacier National Park are just a few of the scenic and historic attractions located nearby. Fishing and scenic pack trips in the Bob Marshall and Mission Mountain Wilderness begin in early July. They are a once-in-a-lifetime experience, yet many take the trips repeatedly.

We are one of Montana's oldest outfitting families with more than 65 years of experience. Our experience and desire to please you combine for a memorable, and we hope, successful trip.

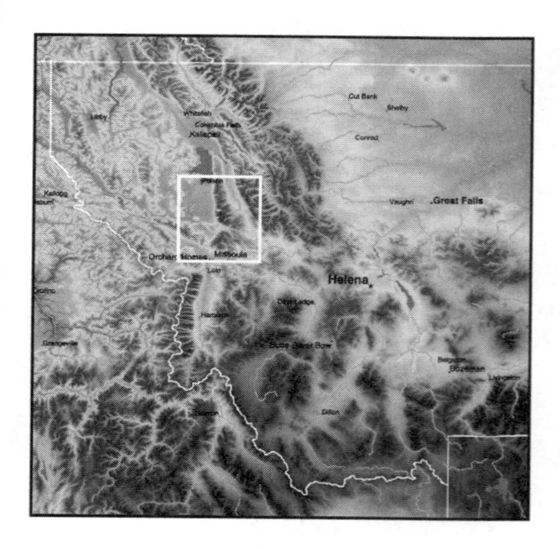

"Their service is outstanding and they always go the extra mile to help in any way." Carol Fisher

SEASONS OF OPERATION

WESTERN ACTIVITIES

ACTIVITIES

SERVICES

CHEFF GUEST
RANCH
Outfitters and Guides

Double Spear Ranch

Tony and Donna Blackmore
P.O. Box 43 • Pryor, MT 59066
phone: (406) 259-8291 • fax: (406) 245-7673
email: DoubleSpearRanch@juno.com

We invite adventurous city slickers to join us and live the real West for a week or two on our working cattle ranch 35 miles south of Billings, Montana, on the Crow Indian Reservation. Although a relative of old Sitting Bull, your cowboss Tony Blackmore will remind you more of John Wayne. Ride the range and the mountains, work cattle, learn colt-breaking and horsemanship techniques, and enjoy cowboy cookouts. You will ride quarter horses and meet rare (hypoallergenic!) American curly horses — buffalo — and lots more livestock and pets. This isn't a fancy upscale vacation; you will join in and experience real ranch life. Expect a little dust, a little sweat, and tons of laughter.

We include your own horse, unlimited riding, ranch meals cowboy-style, airport pickup and delivery. Bedrooms for adults in ranch house or bunkhouse (shared facilities).

Special 2-week western youth camps for guests 13-19.

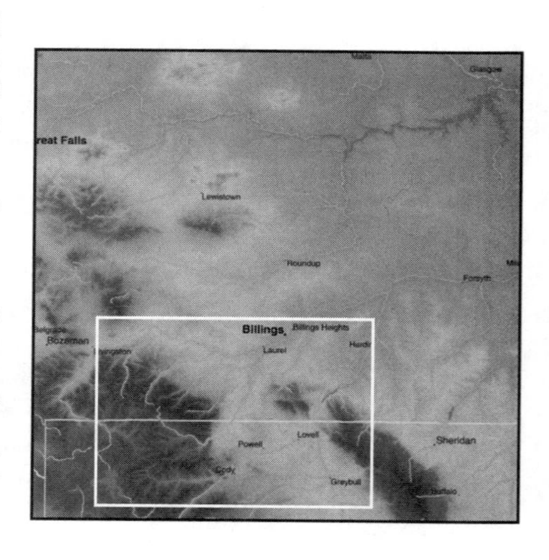

"I had a terrific time. I will go back as soon as I possibly can, it was fantastic!" Rita Young

SEASONS OF OPERATION

WESTERN ACTIVITIES

ACTIVITIES

SERVICES

Esper's Under Wild Skies Lodge & Outfitters

Vaughn and Judy Esper
P.O. Box 849 • Philipsburg, MT 59858
phone: (406) 859-3000 • fax: (406) 859-3161

Under Wild Skies Lodge and Outfitters is located in the Deerlodge National Forest at the boundary of the Anaconda Pintler Wilderness.

Our guest ranch offers something for everyone. For the fisherman we have two lakes on the ranch.

The Middle Fork of Rock Creek traverses through the property and offers four species of trout. Take a scenic wilderness horseback ride for a day or an overnight pack trip into the majestic Pintler Mountains. Or, just relax in the casual elegance of the lodge.

At Under Wild Skies we take pride in our facilities, services, and the meticulous attention we pay to every detail of your stay. You come as a guest and leave as a friend.

"Wonderful experience, beautiful location, great cooking, 'unmatched'!"
Mr. & Mrs. Ronald Vachon

SEASONS OF OPERATION

ACTIVITIES

SERVICES

ESPER'S
LODGE & OUTFITTERS
UNDER
WILD SKIES
MONTANA

EW Watson & Sons Outfitting

Ed and Wanda Watson

7837 U.S. Hwy. 287 • Townsend, MT 59644
phone: (800) 654-2845 • (406) 266-3741 • fax: (406) 266-4498
email: ewwatson@initico.net • www.ewwatson.com

WHERE THE ONLY THING BETTER THAN THE SCENERY IS THE SERVICE

E W Watson & Sons Outfitting is dedicated to providing top hands, quality horses, and an educational and affordable vacation.

Customize your trip to your pleasure. Explore these opportunities: horseback pack-in camping trips; mountain lake fly fishing trips; covered wagon trips; Missouri River float trips; and, authentic working ranch cattle drives.

Combine local historical points of interest with ranch home lodging. Visit Elkhorn Ghost Town, tour Lewis and Clark Caverns, ride the tour train at Helena and learn about the colorful gold rush days.

"Hard working, knowledgeable guides. Great cook and good food. A first rate Outfitter." John K. McKeag

SEASONS OF OPERATION

WESTERN ACTIVITIES

ACTIVITIES

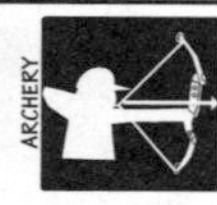

SERVICES

EW

Hargrave Cattle and Guest Ranch

Leo and Ellen Hargrave

300 Thompson River Rd. • Marion, MT 59925
phone: (406) 858-2284 • fax: (406) 858-2444
email: hargrave@digisys.net • www.hargraveranch.com

Live the legend on a historic 87,000 acre working ranch. National forest surrounds our mountain valley jewel. Choose your adventure, whether it's many hours in the saddle or a leisurely ride to check cattle. Join us in spring for calving and herd-check riding. Join summer drives to the range or fall roundups. Count stars on a campout by pristine lake and peaks. Day trips to spectacular Glacier National Park or National Bison Range. Skeet and target shooting, archery, lake canoeing, cowboy campfire sing-a-longs, pool games in the horse barn museum, and private meadow fishing. On-site massage therapist arranged.

Outfitted fly fishing float trips, whitewater rafting, guided fall hunting, winter cross country skiing and holiday cabins. Grandma's cooking, delightful lodging, and caring are our standards.

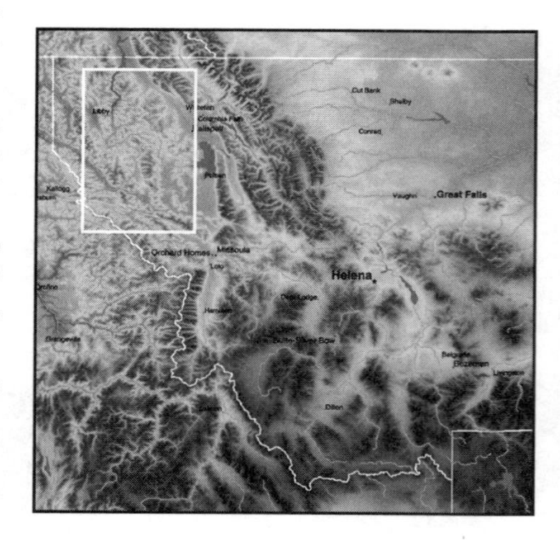

We were Outfitters on the Great Montana Cattle Drive and are committed to sharing that Western Spirit with our guests.

"It was a dream come true - reality was 1,000 times better than the dream. It's the adventure of a lifetime!!!" Virginia Wiscovich

SEASONS OF OPERATION

WESTERN ACTIVITIES

ACTIVITIES

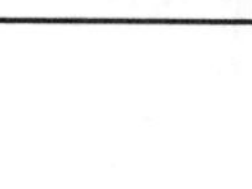

SERVICES

HARGRAVE CATTLE & GUEST RANCH
HARGRAVE
THOMPSON RIVER VALLEY
MARION. MONTANA

HARGRAVE
CHAROLAIS RANCH

Hidden Hollow Hideaway

Kelly and Jill Flynn
P.O. Box 233 • Townsend, MT 59644
phone: (406) 266-3322

Our ranch — more than 20,000 acres of mountains, creeks, meadows, and forests — is known as Hidden Hollow Ranch, home of the Hideaway. On our northern ranch, the Hideaway nestles alongside a meandering stream under towering willow trees. Two acres of landscaped lawns surround the old lodge, log cabin, small cabin and new main lodge. The cabins are rustic but very comfortable. All have showers, electricity, and wood stoves. Three home-cooked meals are served daily.

Ride horses on a ridge overlooking miles of mountains and meadows. Pan for gold alongside a rushing mountain stream. Take an "off the beaten path" four-wheel-drive tour. Sit around a campfire or enjoy a barbecue. Hike through wildflower-blazing meadows. Fish at a nearby creek or one of our ranch ponds. Pitch in on some of the ranch work, or just sit back and enjoy the peace and solitude.

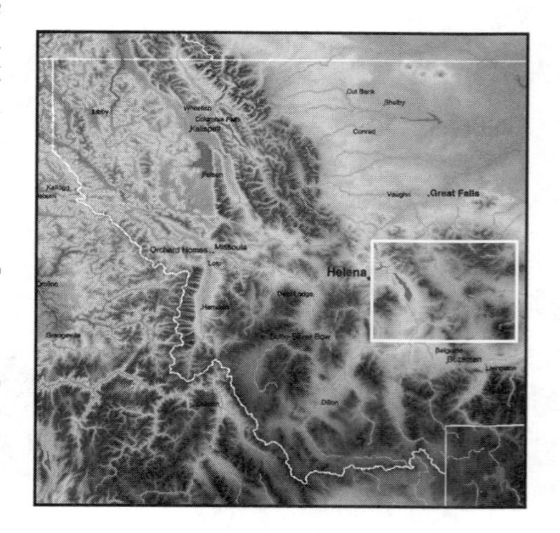

" Kelly Flynn makes it all happen!"
Marion Dial

SEASONS OF OPERATION

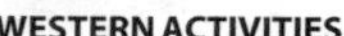

WESTERN ACTIVITIES

ACTIVITIES

SERVICES

Iron Wheel Ranch

John & Sherry Cargill
40 Cedar Hills Road • Whitehall, MT 59759
phone/fax: (406) 494-2960 • mobile: (406) 491-2960

Recreation is a full-time job for our family run business. We offer all forms of summer recreation for everyone. Trail rides for individuals or groups up to 8, hourly or full-day trips with cookouts.

Our youth camps for children 7-15 specialize in teaching children how to handle, saddle, care and ride their horse. Child gets their "own" horse for the entire week. We camp out and children put up their own tent and learn other camping responsibilities.

Blue ribbon rivers are fun for everyone, with many river and fishing options available as well as our private pond.

Our Bed & Breakfast lodge offers many combination vacations including float trips, trail rides, seasonal varmint and big game hunts. On site we have horseshoe pits, volleyball net, BBQ's, fire rings and a creek. We are located near the Continental Divide and easily accessible.

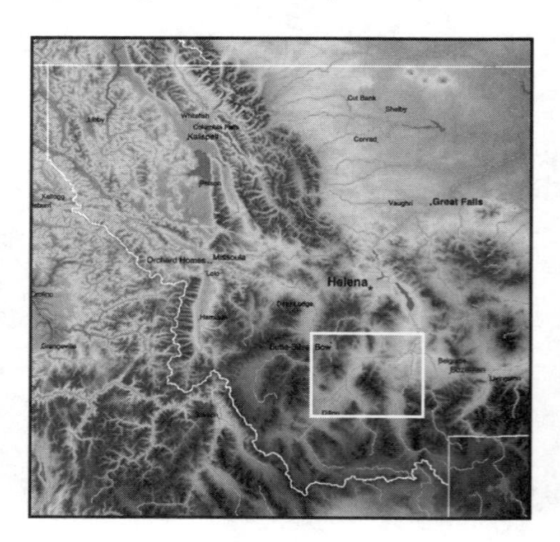

"They go the extra mile to accommodate your desires. They have super accommodations."

SEASONS OF OPERATION

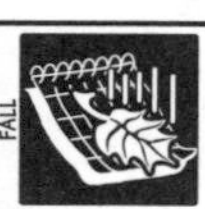

WESTERN ACTIVITIES

ACTIVITIES

SERVICES

IRON WHEEL RANCH
Youth Camps
Trail Rides
Bed-n-Breakfast
Big Game Hunts
Float Trips

Monture Face Outfitters

Tom Ide and Valerie Call
Box 27 • Greenough, MT 59836
phone: (888) 420-5768 • phone/fax: (406) 244-5763
email: info@montanaoutfitter.com • www.montanaoutfitter.com

Monture Face Outfitters is your host to Montana's "Bob Marshall Wilderness," nearly 1.5 million acres of pristine beauty in the heart of the Rocky Mountains.

Travel into and through the wilderness on top-notch horses and mules. Pack trips are flexible, from three days to a high adventure eight-day roving experience. Abundant wildflowers and wildlife provide photo opportunities at every bend of the trail, and the trout fishing is outstanding. Only the highest quality ingredients are used in the gourmet wilderness kitchen. Build campfires at night and immerse yourself in a sea of stars.

Owner Tom Ide, son Tim, and Valerie Call have one ultimate goal; to share the magic of wilderness. Knowledgeable, experienced and quality-oriented.

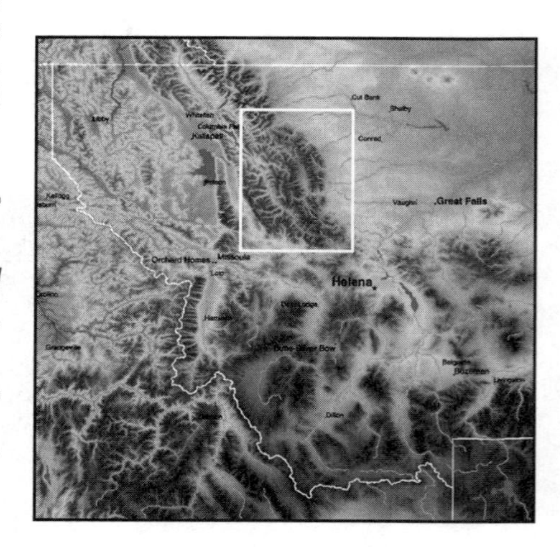

"Everything was well planned and executed. The food was fabulous....I would enthusiastically recommend this outfitter to anyone!" Bill Bailey

SEASONS OF OPERATION

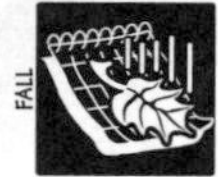

WESTERN ACTIVITIES

ACTIVITIES

SERVICES

MONTURE FACE Outfitters

Monture Face Outfitters

Nine Quarter Circle Guest Ranch

Kim and Kelly Kelsey
5000 Taylor Fork Rd. • Gallatin Gateway, MT 59730
phone: (406) 995-4276 (ranch) • (406) 586-4972 (home)

From a secluded valley overlooking Yellowstone National Park, the Kelseys have been hosting guests for more than 50 years. The ranch-raised herd of 120 Appaloosa horses will take you through pine forests, over mountain streams and across wildflower-strewn meadows. Fun at the Nine Quarter includes children with a kiddie wrangler and a ranch babysitter. Among the weekly activities are square dances, hay rides, wildlife lectures and softball games. Other pastimes include hiking, photography or just relaxing on your porch to the cry of a coyote.

The Taylor Fork, a fine trout stream, flows through the ranch. With a trout pond and ranch guide at your side, you will soon be hooked on fishing these famous headwaters of the Missouri River.

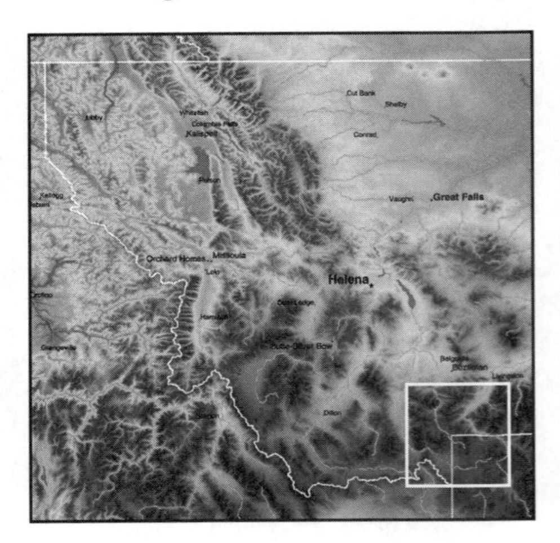

"Our vacation in Montana has become a family tradition, to go back to 'the ranch, our ranch' Nine Quarter Circle Ranch, Gallatin Gateway, Montana." Mr. & Mrs. Brian Hensley

SEASONS OF OPERATION

WESTERN ACTIVITIES

ACTIVITIES

SERVICES

Nine Quarter Guest Ranch

Rich Ranch

Jack and Belinda Rich
P.O. Box 495 • Seeley Lake, MT 59868
phone: (406) 677-2317 • fax: (406) 677-3530
email: richranch@montana.com • www.richranch.com

Summer ranch vacations are available from May through September. While at the ranch you will enjoy quiet country living. The lodge and cabins are nestled in the trees overlooking a large natural meadow with a scenic backdrop of majestic mountains. We are surrounded by more than one million acres of state and national forests.

Horseback riding is the main activity. Each guest is fitted to a saddle and we carefully choose a horse suited to your ability. Do you prefer a leisurely morning ride through the meadows and rolling hills, a high adventure trip to the top of the mountain, or maybe some time to work on your horsemanship skills in our outdoor arena? The choice is yours. Quality fishing for all levels, beginner to expert, is available in nearby lakes, streams and rivers.

"I would have to say our enthusiasm from our trip was infectious enough that other couples and an acquaintance asked to go along on our next trip!" John L. Trudel

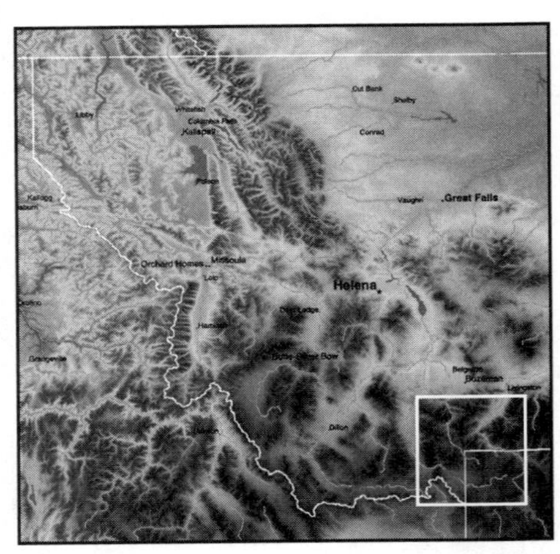

SEASONS OF OPERATION

WESTERN ACTIVITIES

ACTIVITIES

SERVICES

Rich Ranch

Three Cross Ranch

Dan and Arleene Weppler
1281 Hines Ranch Road • Ryegate, MT 59074-9401
phone: (4060) 568-2280 • fax: (406) 663-2100
email: tcr@midrivers.com • www.threecrossranch.com

Enjoy a touch of the "Old West". Our "Wagon Train/Cattledrive/Trailride" is designed to take you back to a time in history to live the life of the 'cattledrive cowboy'. Experience a bit of what it was like when cowboys trailed cattle from Texas to Montana in the 1800's.

What can you expect? Horseback riding, moving cattle, and wildlife viewing. Meals prepared from a true "chuckwagon": Bar-B-Q's (featuring beef and bison) and campfire cookouts. You'll sleep under the "Big Sky" in a cowboy bedroll using your saddle for a pillow. You will have time to reflect and listen to the howl of coyotes or the hooting of an owl. View Indian artifacts and petroglyphs. Fish, rock hunt, bird watch, swim, and even fix fence! Share the good times. Tell stories and tales around a campfire in the late evening. Share your day's experiences and anticipate the next day's adventures!

Welcome to the Three Cross Ranch!

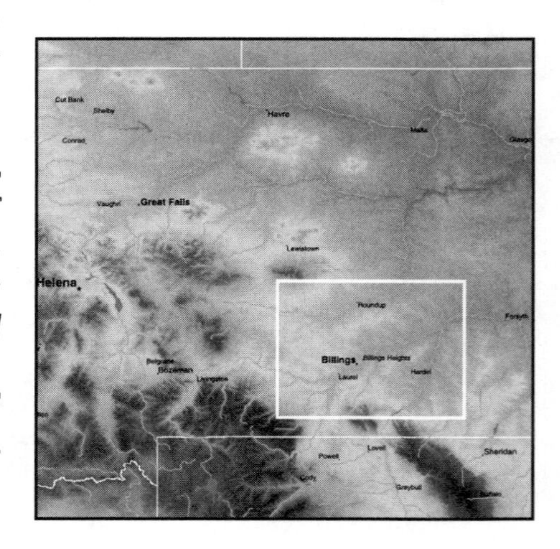

"Dan & Arleene have such a love and respect for the land. It was a fantastic experience for us all, especially my children to experience a real western-type adventure. I can't say enough good about them!" Brent Sorensen, Graham, WA

SEASONS OF OPERATION

WESTERN ACTIVITIES

ACTIVITIES

SERVICES

WTR Outfitters

Karen Hooker

520 Cooper Lake Rd. • Ovando, MT 59854
phone: (800) 987-5666 • phone/fax: (406) 793-5666
email: wtroutfitters@montana.com • www.wtroutfitters.com

WTR Outfitters has been specializing in summer horse pack trips since 1940.

Join Karen Hooker and and her crew on the ride of a lifetime into the Bob Marshall, Great Bear and ScapegoatWilderness areas.

Hike across fields splashed with the bright blues, reds and yellows of alpine flowers. Ride along the Chinese Wall, a 1,500 foot sheer cliff.

Fish for native cutthroat trout in remote, gin-clear streams. Photograph deer, elk, and perhaps even a grizzly.

Trips can be customized to suit your wishes or you can join one of our scheduled trips.

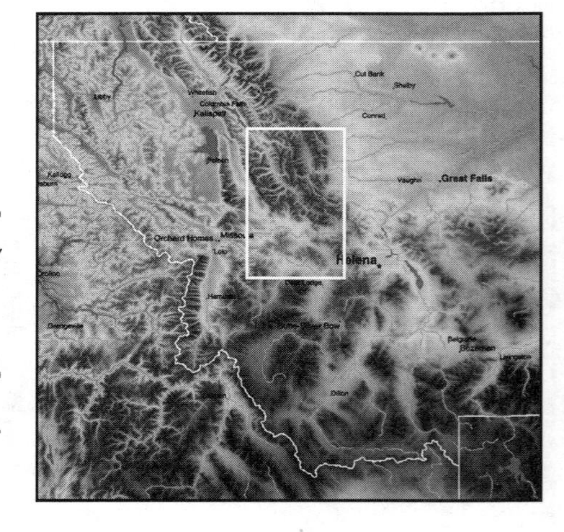

"In my opinion the Hookers are the very top of their profession!"
John & Rose Marie McGoldrick

SEASONS OF OPERATION

WESTERN ACTIVITIES

ACTIVITIES

SERVICES

Top Rated Professionals in

New Mexico

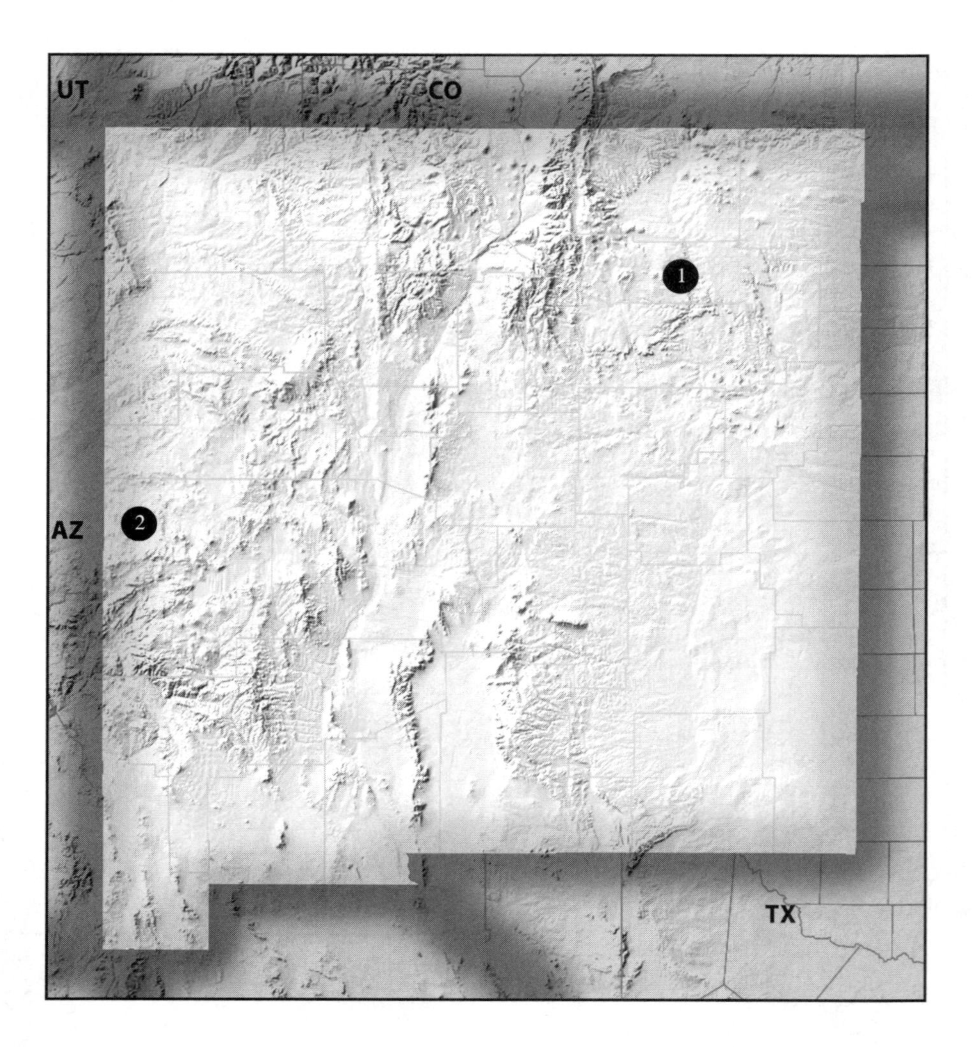

Outdoor Professionals

1. Hartley Guest Ranch
2. Maynard Ranch

License and Report Requirements

- State requires that Hunting Outfitters be licensed.
- State requires the filing of an "Annual Report of Outfitters' Clients" for hunting only.
- "Use Permit" required for Fish and River Outfitters using BLM and Forest Service lands. They are not required to file any reports.

Useful information for the state of

New Mexico

State and Federal Agencies

New Mexico Fish and Game
PO Box 25112
Santa Fe, NM 87504
phone: (505) 827-7911
fax: (505) 827-7915

General Info & Proclamation Requests
(800) 862-9310

Forest Service
Southwestern Region
Federal Building
517 Gold Avenue SW
Albuquerque, NM 87102
phone: (505) 842-3300
TTY: (505) 842-3898

Carson National Forest
phone: (505) 758-6200

Cibola National Forest
phone / TTY: (505) 761-4650

Gila National Forest
phone: (505) 388-8201

Lincoln National Forest
phone: (505) 434-7200

Santa Fe National Forest
phone: (505) 438-7840

Bureau of Land Management
New Mexico State Office
1474 Rodeo Road
Santa Fe, NM 87505

Mailing Address:
P.O. Box 27115
Santa Fe, NM 87502-0115

Information Number: (505) 438-7400
fax: (505) 438-7435
Office Hours: 7:45 a.m. - 4:30 p.m.

National Parks

Carlsbad Caverns National Park
3225 National Parks Hwy.
Carlsbad, NM 88220
phone: (505) 785-2232
Email: cave_interpretation@nps.gov

Associations, Publications, etc.

DudeRanches.com
http://www.duderanches.com

American Fisheries Society
New Mexico Chapter
C. Marc Wethington
New Mexico Dept. of Fish & Game
PO Box 6429
Navajo Dam, NM 87419
phone: (505) 623-8818 or (505) 827-7915

Federation of Fly Fishers
http://www.fedflyfishers.org

Trout Unlimited Rio Grande Chapter
President: Michael Norte
7849 Quintana NE
Albuquerque, NM 87109
phone: (505) 844-0935

New Mexico Bass Chapter Federation
PO Box 717
Socorro, NM 87801
phone: (505) 835-1200

New Mexico Council of Outfitters & Guides, Inc.
160 Washington SE #75
Albuquerque, NM 87108
phone: (505) 764-2670

Hartley Guest Ranch

Doris and Ray Hartley
HCR 73, Box 55 • Roy, NM 87743
phone: (800) OUR-DUDE (687-3833) • (505) 673-2245 • fax: (505) 673-2216
email: rhart@etsc.net • www.duderanch.org/hartley

So, should you have been a cowboy? The Hartley Family invites you to experience and enjoy our working cattle ranch, nestled in the breathtaking beauty of New Mexico.

Explore 200 miles of trails that circle the rims of redrock canyons and wind through forest of juniper, oak and pine by horseback or ATV.

Other ranch activities: cattle working, branding, campouts, fishing, campfires, and hiking. Discover ancient Indian sites, dinosaur bones, and unusual geological formations located on the ranch. Rafting trips and day trips to enchanting Santa Fe and Taos.

Delicious home-cooked meals are served family-style in the dining room or cooked outdoors over an open fire. Transportation from Albuquerque.

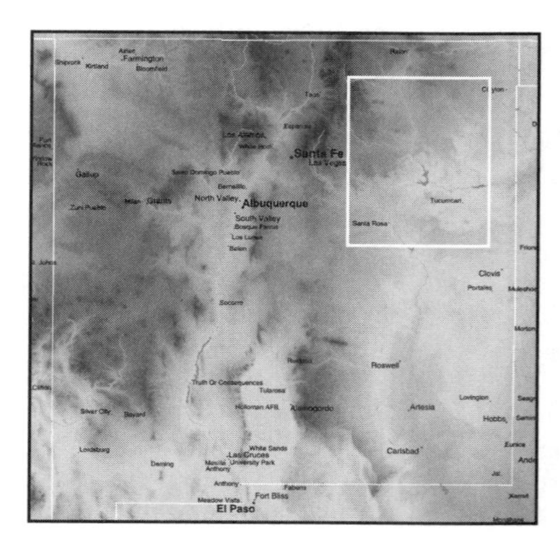

"The trip was a 'once in a lifetime' experience that I'd like to repeat many times!"
Catherine Kaplus

SEASONS OF OPERATION

WESTERN ACTIVITIES

ACTIVITIES

SERVICES

Maynard Ranch

Perry and Brenda Hunsaker • Billy and Nora Maynard
19831 E Warner Rd. • Higley, AZ 85236
phone: (602) 988-9654 • fax: (602) 988-3292
email: outwest@maynardranch.com • www.maynardranch.com

You're invited to spend some time at an authentic New Mexico cattle and guest ranch. Roam the mountains and valleys where some of the West's most famous outlaws stirred up havoc, including Billy the Kid and Butch Cassidy.

Set on nearly 3,000 acres and surrounded by National Forest with towering ponderosa pines, oak thickets and lush meadows. Enjoy horseback riding through the forests or spend time in the saddle with cowboys working cattle. Play cowboy golf, take a hayride, go fishing or just sit back and unwind. Daytrips available to nearby Indian ruins and archaeological sites. Spend evenings around the campfire listening to a cowboy poet or enjoy the star-filled sky and Milky Way. We offer a great kids' program.

The ranch has comfortable accommodations perfect for family reunions and corporate retreats. Hearty meals are served family-style.

"The food was delicious, and the coffee pot was always going. A total warm & relaxing experience. Can't wait to return to Maynard Ranch!" Carol Jordan

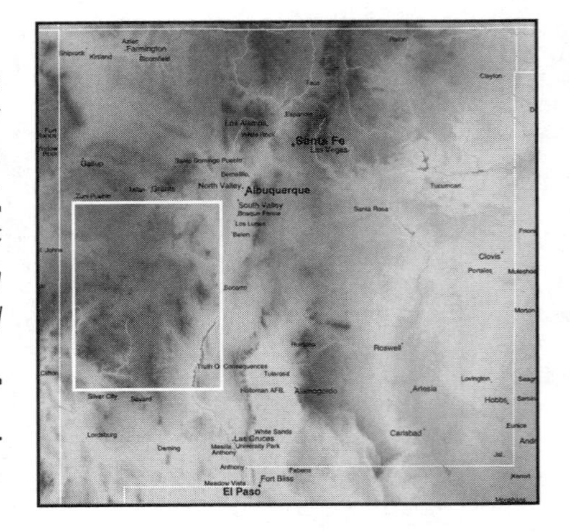

SEASONS OF OPERATION

WESTERN ACTIVITIES

ACTIVITIES

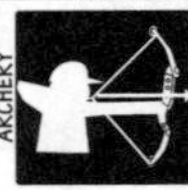

SERVICES

RANCH TIMBERLINE OUTFITTER
POSTED

Top Rated Professionals in

North Carolina

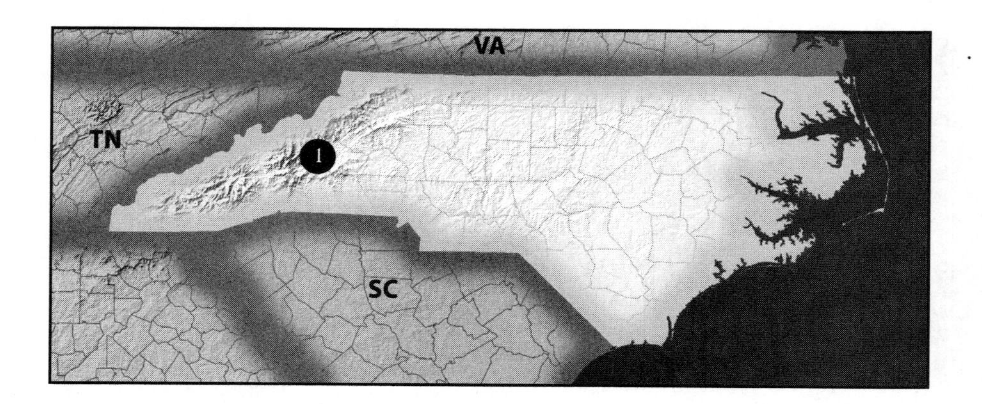

Outdoor Professionals

1 Clear Creek Guest Ranch

License and Report Requirements

- State does not license or register Outfitters, Guides, Captains or Lodges.
- State has no report requirements.

Useful information for the state of

North Carolina

State and Federal Agencies

North Carolina Wildlife Resources Commission
Archdale Building
512 N. Salisbury St.
Raleigh, NC 27611
(919) 733-3391

Marine Fisheries
(919) 726-7021

Bureau of Land Management
Eastern States
7450 Boston Boulevard
Springfield, Virginia 22153
Phone: (703) 440-1600
or (703) 440- Plus Extension
Fax: (703) 440-1599

Office Hours: 8:00 a.m. - 4:30 p.m.

Eastern States
Jackson Field Office
411 Briarwood Drive, Suite 404
Jackson, Mississippi 39206
Phone: (601) 977-5400
Fax: (601) 977-5440

Forest Service
Southern Region
1720 Peachtree Road NW
Atlanta, GA 30367
phone: (404) 347-4177
TTY: (404) 347-4278

Croatan-Nantahala-Pisgah-Uwharrie National Forests
phone: (704) 257-4200

Associations, Publications, etc.

DudeRanches.com
http://www.duderanches.com

American Fisheries Society
Box 7617
NC State University
Raleigh, NC 27695
phone: (919) 515-2631

Trout Unlimited North Carolina
135 Tacoma Circle
Asheville, NC 28801-1625
phone: (704) 684-5178
fax: (704) 687-1689

National Hunters Association, Inc.
PO Box 820
Knightdale, NC 27545
phone: (919) 365-7157

Professional Bowhunters Society
PO Box 246
Terrell, NC 28682
phone/fax: (704) 664-2534

Carolina Bird Club, Inc.
PO Box 29555
Raleigh, NC 27626-0555

North Carolina Bass Chapter Federation
1105 Misty Wood Lane
Harrisburg, NC 28075
phone: (704) 785-9108

Clear Creek Guest Ranch

Rex Frederick
100 Clear Creek Rd., Hwy. 80 South • Burnsville, NC 28714
phone: (800) 651-4510 • (704) 675-4510 • fax: (704) 675-5452
email: clearcreek@mcwalters.net • www.clearcreekranch.com

"Best vacation ever! Just like family. ... A piece of heaven. ... Wonderful time, great staff, we'll be back!" These are just a few of the notes we've received from recent guests.

Our goal at CCR is to give you the most relaxing, yet fun-filled vacation possible. Rooms are cozily furnished with lodgepole pine furniture, quilts and all are carpeted, air-conditioned and heated. All buildings have big porches with rockers and offer a magnificent view of the Black Mountains.

Activities include horseback riding, trout fishing, hiking, whitewater rafting and tubing on the South Toe River. A highlight of our week is the Saturday "rodeo."

Come and see for yourself. Clear Creek Ranch brings a bit of the Old West to the mountains of North Carolina. Call for a brochure and more details.

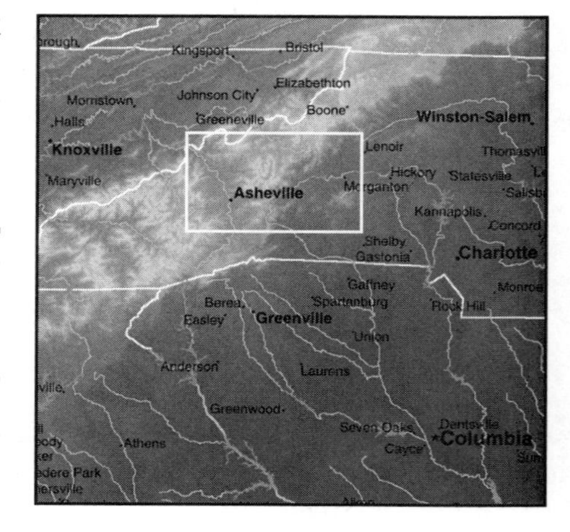

"It was truly the best vacation ever. Better than Disney World!"
Mr. and Mrs. John Ludlum

SEASONS OF OPERATION

WESTERN ACTIVITIES

ACTIVITIES

SERVICES

CLEAR CREEK
GUEST RANCH

Top Rated Professionals in

North Dakota

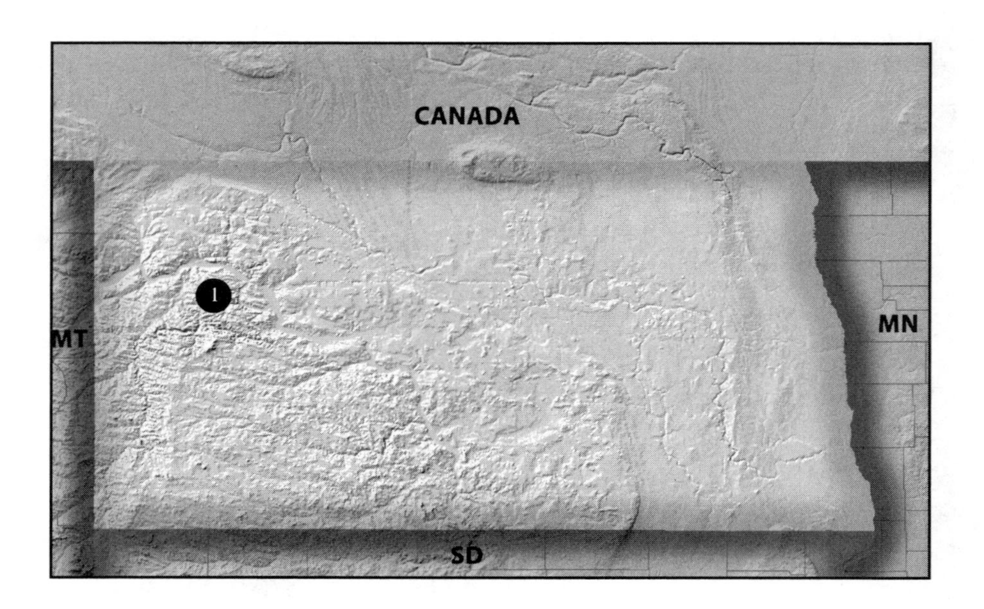

Outdoor Professionals

❶ Little Knife Outfitters

License and Report Requirements

- State licenses all guides: hunting, fishing, trapping, river, etc. All guides are required to keep reports but are not required to submit them.

Useful information for the state of

North Dakota

State and Federal Agencies

North Dakota Game & Fish Dept.
100 North Bismarck Expressway
Bismarck, ND 58501
(701) 328-6300
fax: (701) 328-6352

Bureau of Land Management
Montana State Office
(serves North & South Dakota also)
222 North 32nd Street
P.O. Box 36800
Billings, Montana 59107-6800

Phone: (406) 255-2885
Fax: (406) 255-2762
Email - mtinfo@mt.blm.gov

Dakotas District Office
2933 Third Avenue West
Dickinson, North Dakota 58601-2619
Phone: (701) 225-9148
Fax: (701) 227-8510
Email - ddomail@mt.blm.gov

Office Hours: 8:00 a.m. - 4:30 p.m.

State Forest Service
307 First Street
Bottineau, ND 58318-1100
phone: (701) 228-5422
fax: (701) 228-5448

National Parks

Theodore Roosevelt National Park
Medora, ND 58645
phone: (701) 623-4466

Associations, Publications, etc.

DudeRanches.com
http://www.duderanches.com

Dakota Outdoors
PO Box 669
Pierre, SD 57501-0669
Phone: (605) 224-7301
Fax: (605) 224-9210

American Fisheries Society
South Dakota Council
RR 1, Box 205
Spearfish, SD 57783-8905
phone: (605) 642-6920
fax: (605) 692-6921

Federation of Fly Fishers
http://www.fedflyfishers.org

Little Knife Outfitters

Glendon "Swede" Nelson

RR 1, Box 116 • Stanley, ND 58784
phone: 701-628-2747 • fax: 701-628-3254
email: swede@4u.net • http://www.4eyes.net/littleknife/default.htm

Would you enjoy an authentic western adventure in the backcountry? Would you enjoy a real cowboy experience replete with horses, campsites, western-style meals, beautiful sunrises, sunsets, wildlife, and nature? If you answered "yes" to these questions, allow us to introduce ourselves.

We are Swede and Jean Nelson, owners and operators of Little Knife Outfitters. We offer one- to six-day trail ride adventures during June, July and August. We outfit our clients with riding supplies, serve them western-style meals, and guide their excursion through the North Unit of the Theodore Roosevelt National Park in western North Dakota. Our adventure takes us through 24,000 acres of wilderness and secluded backcountry complete with authentic Indian and cowboy cultural artifacts from the days of westward expansion. Our regularly-scheduled or tailor-made rides depart from the banks of the Little Missouri River.

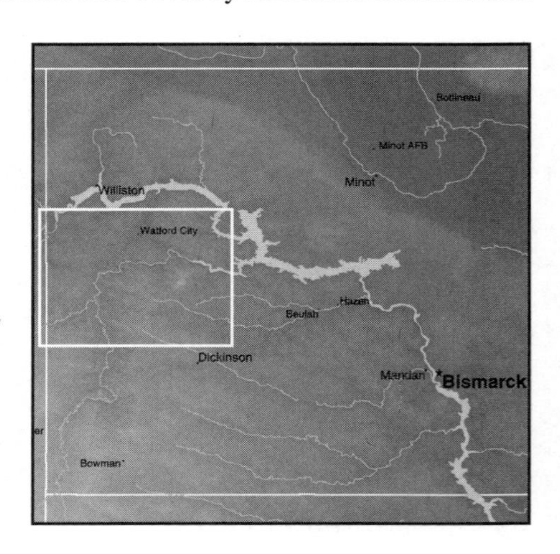

"I have taken my employees on this ride twice. We all forget the pressure of the business world and communicate to each other about 'real topics' of life. Great time, can't wait to do it again" Roger Gjeiistad-Stanley Equipment, Inc.

SEASONS OF OPERATION

SUMMER 

WESTERN ACTIVITIES

HORSEBACK  HORSE PACK TRIPS  CATTLE DRIVES 

ACTIVITIES

ARCHEOLOGICAL SITES 

SERVICES

CABINS  WALL TENTS  FAMILY  FULL BOARD  GUIDED ACTIVITIES  DAY TRIPS  OVERNIGHT TRIPS

Little Knife Outfitters, Inc.

Top Rated Professionals in

Oregon

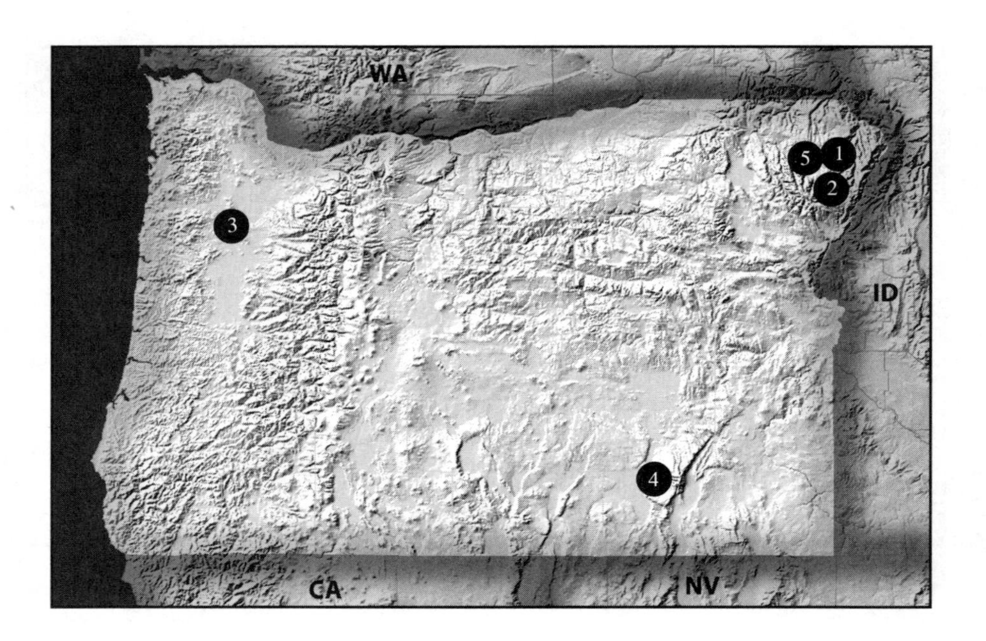

Outdoor Professionals

1. Cornucopia Wilderness Pack Station, Inc.
2. Outback Ranch Outfitters
3. S.A.L.E.M. Treks - Wiley Woods Ranch
4. Steens Mountain Packers
5. Wallowa Llamas

License and Report Requirements

- State requires licensing of Outdoor Professionals.
- State requires a "Year-End Report" for Outfitters hunting and/or fishing on BLM land.
- U.S. Coast Guard licensing required for guides and captains that fish in "Near Coastal Waters".

Useful information for the state of

Oregon

State and Federal Agencies

Oregon Dept. of Fish & Wildlife
PO Box 59
Portland, OR 97207
phone: (503) 872-5268

Oregon Marine Board
435 Commercial St. NE
Salem, OR 97310
phone: (503) 373-1405
or (503) 378-8587

Columbia River Gorge Ntl. Scenic Area
902 Wasco Avenue, Ste 200
Hood River, OR 97031
phone: (541) 386-2333

Forest Service
Pacific Northwest Region
333 SW 1st Avenue, PO Box 3623
Portland, OR 97208
phone: (503) 326-2971
TTY: (503) 326-6448

Rogue River National Forest
phone: (541) 858-2200

Siskiyou National Forest
phone: (541) 471-6500

Siuslaw National Forest
phone: (541) 750-7000

Umpqua National Forest
phone: (541) 672-6601

Winema National Forest
phone: (541) 883-6714

Bureau of Land Management
Oregon State Office
1515 SW 5th Ave., P.O. Box 2965
Portland, OR 97208-2965
phone: (503) 952-6001
or (503) 952-Plus Extension
fax: (503) 952-6308
Tdd: (503) 952-6372

Electronic mail
General Information:
or912mb@or.blm.gov
Webmaster: orwww@or.blm.gov

National Parks

Crater Lake National Park
phone: (541) 594-2211

Associations, Publications, etc.

American Fisheries Society
19948 S. Leland Road
Oregon City, OR 97045
phone: (503) 731-1267
fax: (503) 235-4228

Oregon Trout, Inc.
117 SW Front Ave.
Portland, OR 97204
phone: (503) 222-9091

Trout Unlimited Oregon Council
22875 NW Chestnut Street
Hillsboro, OR 97124-6545
phone: (541) 640-2123
fax: (503) 844-9929

Federation of Fly Fishers
http://www.fedflyfishers.org

Oregon Bass Chapter Federation
2475 N. Baker Drive
Canby, OR 97013
phone: (503) 266-7729

Oregon Outdoor Association
PO Box 9486
Bend, OR 97708-9486
phone: (541) 382-9758

Cornucopia Wilderness Pack Station

Eldon and Marge Deardorff
Rt. 1, Box 50 • Richland, OR 97870
phone: (541) 893-6400 • summer camp: (541) 742-5400

Cornucopia Wilderness Pack Station, Inc., brings you back to nature. Located in the high country of the Eagle Cap Wilderness Area (not far from where *Paint Your Wagon* was filmed) it is nestled among the pines in the ghost town of Cornucopia, a gold mining boom town in its day.

The operators are natives of the area and have complete and competent knowledge of the guide and packing business.

The pack station is used by everyone — from the avid hunter and fisherman to groups and families just wanting to get away from the hustle and bustle of the everyday life. First-timers right out of the city are in for one of the biggest thrills they will ever experience.

Much of our business is derived from satisfied returning customers. We are sure you will be one of them.

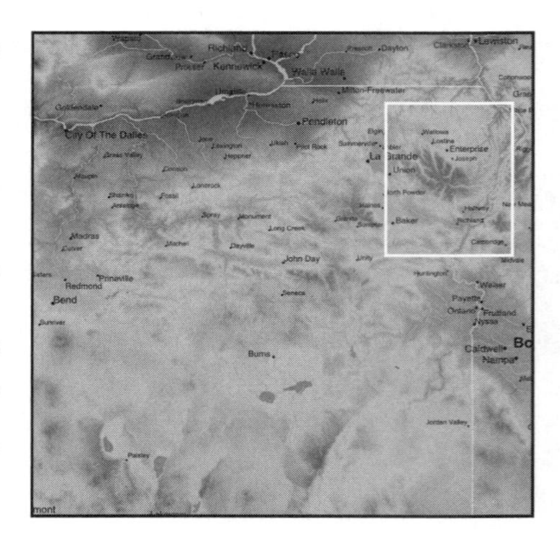

"We will give them an A+ on everything, especially the food." Mavis & Ernest Grellert

SEASONS OF OPERATION

WESTERN ACTIVITIES

ACTIVITIES

SERVICES

Cornucopia Wilderness Pack Station

Outback Ranch Outfitters

Jon and Tracie Wick
P.O. Box 269 • Joseph, OR 97846
phone/fax: (541) 886-2029
www.catsback.com/outbackranch/

Horseback Vacations

Come relax and experience the peace and tranquility of the vast wilderness. The vacation of a lifetime awaits you in one of the following wilderness areas: Eagle Cap, Snake River of Hells Canyon, or the Wenaha-Tucannon.

Horseback riding, fishing, and hunting are available in all areas.

On our most popular summer trips we spend five days flyfishing and sightseeing the more isolated sections of the mountains — an unforgettable trip.

Just pack your clothes, sleeping bag, fishing equipment and personal gear into a duffel bag and come escape the cities and traffic jams. Leave your telephone behind and become a cowboy for a week.

Happy trails.

"I would highly recommend them for anyone looking for fun and adventure. One caution though....be prepared to come back every year!" Jon Peyton

SEASONS OF OPERATION

WESTERN ACTIVITIES

ACTIVITIES

SERVICES

Outback Ranch Outfitters

S.A.L.E.M. Treks—Wiley Woods Ranch

Ken Ploeser
555 Howell Prairie Rd. SE • Salem, OR 97301
phone/fax: (503) 362-0873
email: MPlozr@aol.com • www.oregonlink.com/llama/

Imagine the silence in the deep forest. Gentle winds comb through 100 foot Douglas firs, a fawn dances through tall fern meadows, and you hear a soothing "hummm" from your trail companion — a llama!

Known for their ability to effortlessly carry your load, llamas are the ultimate trail companions. Youngsters and seniors, the physically challenged and hiking enthusiasts all enjoy working closely with these wonderful creatures.

Day treks are customized to meet your physical requirements and schedule. We guide you through the forest of Oregon's beautiful Silver Falls State Park, meandering through the ancient watershed of Silver Creek.

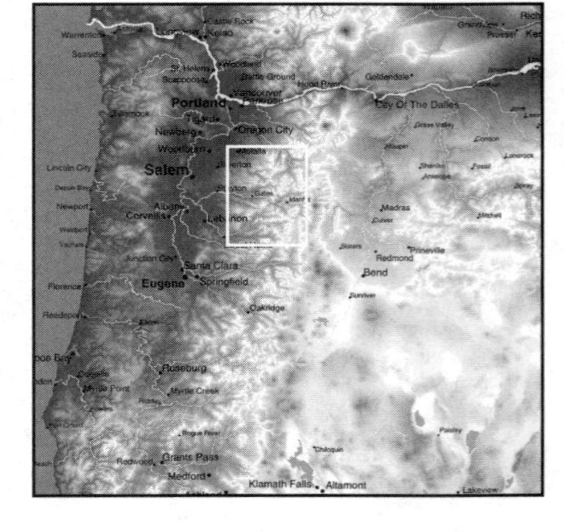

Boasting of 14 breathtaking waterfalls and the historic South Falls Lodge, Silver Falls State Park also offers full hookup and tent campsites, rental cabins, family picnic areas, horse rentals and bike trails.

"It was a lot of fun and the llamas were fun as well as funny!" Susan Mallorie

SEASONS OF OPERATION

WESTERN ACTIVITIES

ACTIVITIES

SERVICES

Steens Mountain Packers

John and Cindy Witzel
Highway 205 • HC 72 Box 71 • Frenchglen, OR 97736
phone: (800) 977-3995
email: info@steensmountain.com • www.steensmountain.com

One of Oregon's protected areas, the Steens Mountain Recreation Lands is an incredible 147,000 acres of deep aspen groves and open meadows, glacial-cut valleys and sheer cliffs, lakes and mountain streams so clear it's unreal.

Wilderness Pack Trips: We offer premier wilderness adventure in our horsepack trips. Explore the unique glaciated terrain laced with an incredible variety of wildflowers while having a true wilderness experience. **Old Style Horse Drive:** We'll be moving our large herd of horses from their winter range to their summer range in much the same way Pete French, a historic cattleman, did back in the late 1800's. Learn the ropes of being a "Loose String Rider". **Cattle Roundup & Drive:** Yes, it's the real thing! Saddle up! We've got cattle to gather out of the high country and head them for their winter range. Hundreds of cattle in thousands of acres are waiting. This is an experience you will carry with you the rest of your life.

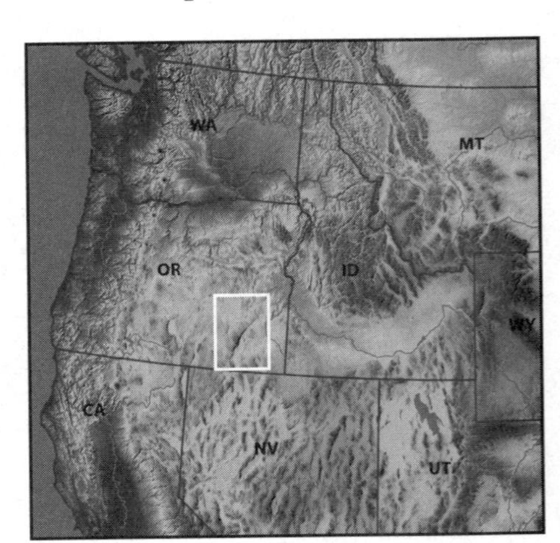

"The Witzel Family are outstanding hosts & Guides. It was the experience of a lifetime. Everyone should try it at least once! We can't wait to go back!" Kathleen Benyak

SEASONS OF OPERATION

WESTERN ACTIVITIES

ACTIVITIES

SERVICES

Wallowa Llamas

Raz and Louise Rasmussen • Steve Backstrom
Rt. 1 Box 84 • Halfway, OR 97834
phone: (541) 742-2961
email: wallama@pdx.oneworld.com

Since 1985, Wallowa Llamas has conducted guided tours of small groups into the state's largest wilderness area, the Eagle Cap.

Here, at the southern edge of Eastern Oregon's spectacular Wallowa Mountains, amid towering peaks, glacier-sculpted valleys and sparkling mountain streams, our llamas carry the amenities, unburdening hikers to experience ease and luxury normally unavailable to backcountry travelers in such rugged environs. Packing with even-tempered llamas, we can enjoy delightful meals prepared without freeze-dried ingredients. Wallowa Llamas provides tents, eating utensils, and all meals, beginning with lunch the first day and ending with lunch the last day.

The llamas will carry up to 20 pounds of each guest's personal gear. Anything above that must be carried by the guest. A daypack is highly recommended for carrying cameras, binoculars or rain gear.

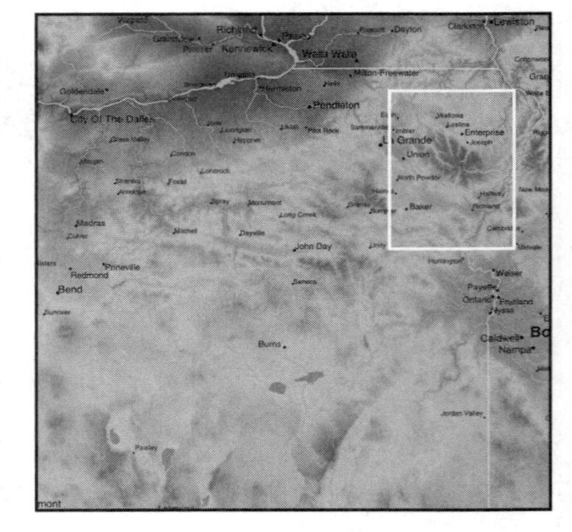

"One of the highlights of my life."
Deanna Watkins

SEASONS OF OPERATION

WESTERN ACTIVITIES

ACTIVITIES

SERVICES

Wallowa Llamas

Top Rated Professionals in

Wyoming

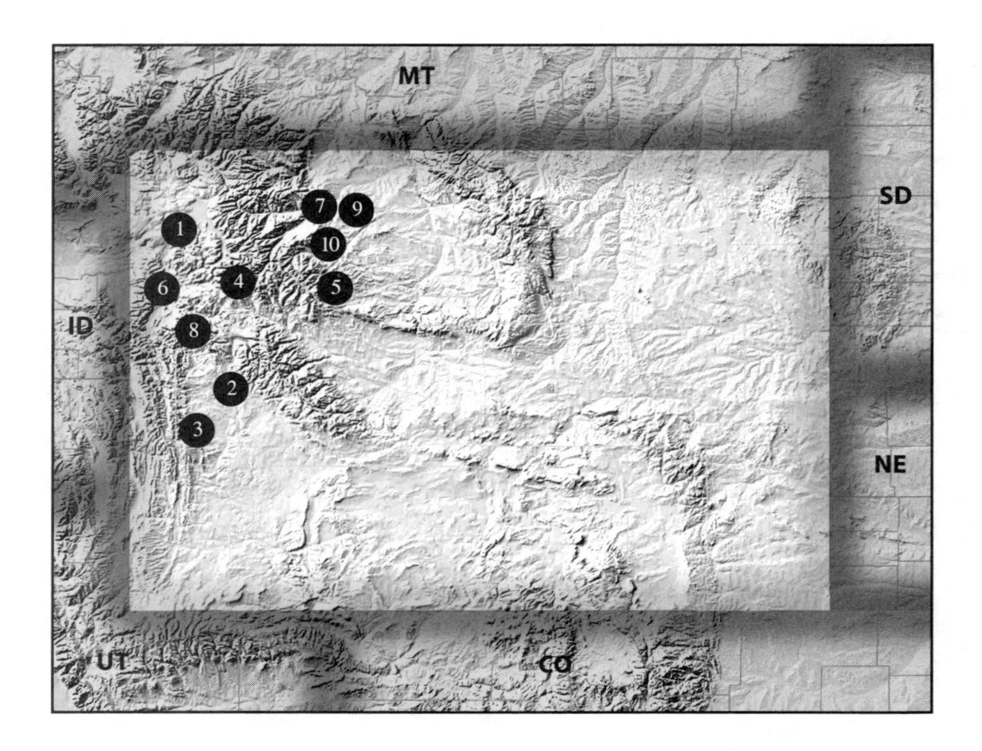

Outdoor Professionals

1. Absaroka Ranch
2. Boulder Lake Lodge
3. Darby Mountain Outfitters
4. Darwin Ranch
5. Early Guest Ranch
6. John Henry Lee Outfitters, Inc.
7. K Bar Z Guest Ranch & Outfitters
8. Lozier's Box "R" Ranch
9. Paintrock Adventures, LLC
10. Triangle C Ranch

Useful information for the state of

Wyoming

State and Federal Agencies

Wyoming Dept. of Admin. & Information
State Board of
Outfitters & Professional Guides
1750 Westland Rd.
Cheyenne, WY 82002
(800) 264-0981
phone: (307) 777-5323
fax: (307) 777-6715

Wyoming Game & Fish Dept.
5400 Bishop Blvd.
Cheyenne, WY 82002
phone: (307) 777-4600

Forest Service
Intermountain Region
Federal Building
324 25th Street
Ogden, UT 84401-2310
phone: (801) 625-5306
TTY: (801) 625-5307

Bridger-Teton National Forests
Forest Service Building
340 North Cache
PO Box 1888
Jackson, WY 83001
phone: (307) 739-5500
TTY: (307) 739-5064

Bureau of Land Management
Wyoming State Office
(serves Nebraska also)
Information Access Center
5353 Yellowstone, P.O. Box 1828
Cheyenne, WY 82003
phone: (307) 775-6BLM or 6256
fax: (307) 775-6082
Office Hours: 7:45 a.m. - 4:30 p.m.

National Parks

Grand Teton National Park
PO Drawer 170
Moose, WY 83012
phone: (307) 739-3399

Yellowstone National Park
PO Box 168
Yellowstone National Park, WY 82190
phone: (307) 344-7381

Associations, Publications, etc.

DudeRanches.com
http://www.duderanches.com

Jackson Hole Chamber of Commerce
PO Box E
Jackson Hole, WY 83001
phone: (307) 733-3316
jhchamber@sisna.com

Jackson Hole Mountain Resort
Teton Village, WY 83025
phone: (800) 443-6931
info@jacksonhole.com

Wyoming Outfitters & Guides Assoc.
PO Box 2284
239 Yellowstone Ave., Suite C
Cody, WY 82414
phone: (307) 527-7453
fax: (307) 587-8633

Jackson Hole Outfitters & Guide
Association
850 W. Broadway
Jackson Hole, WY 83001
phone: (307) 734-9025

License and Report Requirements

- State requires licensing of Outdoor Professionals.
- State requires that Big Game Outfitters file a "Year-End Report".
- Fishing Outfitters need to get a permit to operate on Federal land.
- Outfitters and Guest/Dude Ranches must file a "Use" or "Day Report" with the Wyoming Forest Service if they Fish, Hunt or Raft on Forest Service or BLM land.
- Licensed guides must be signed on and validated by a state licensed outfitter/guide service.

Absaroka Ranch

Robert B. Betts, Jr.

Star Route • Dubois, WY 82513

phone: (307) 455-2275 • www.wyoming.com/~dte/guest-ranch/absaroka

Travel with us by horseback into the largest intact Wilderness area in the lower 48 states. This special country, home of many of the great mountain ranges of the West: the Tetons, the Wind Rivers, and the Absarokas. The scenery is nothing less than spectacular.

The activities are varied and exciting: riding in search of wildlife; picnicking upon the grandest of high-country vistas - the Continental Divide; hiking into a patch of Rocky Mountain wildflowers as multicolored as an artist's palette; fishing for cutthroat, brook, and rainbow trout in the cool, dark holes of the nearby river or creek. This is the land of the famous Mountain Men and many Indian tribes. You'll enjoy the Wilderness in near luxury; clean, dry, spacious tents, warm soft sleeping bags, hearty and varied campfire cooking, and, be guided by some of the most experienced guides and packers in the region. Our horses are completely gentle and mountain wise. A rider of any age, with little or no previous experience, can learn quickly and easily.

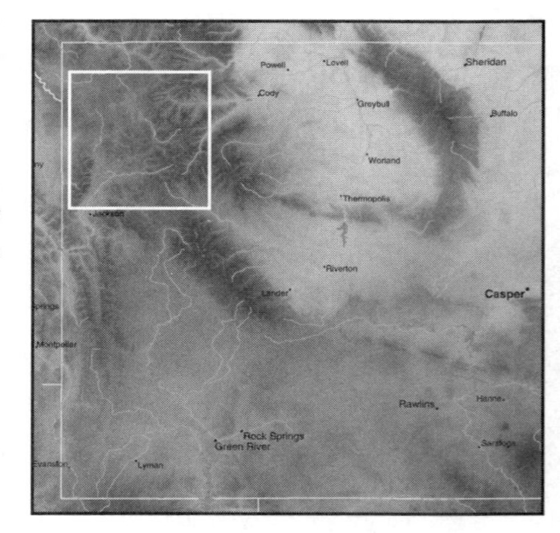

"This was a fabulous experience. One of the best vacations we have ever taken!"
Stuart Kaufman, Great Neck, NY

SEASONS OF OPERATION

WESTERN ACTIVITIES

ACTIVITIES

SERVICES

Boulder Lake Lodge

Kim Bright
Box 1100H • Pinedale, WY 82941
phone: (800) 788-5401 • (307) 537-5400

Boulder Lake Lodge, located on the west slope of the remote and rugged Wind River Mountain Range, serves as headquarters for our many varied pack trip operations.

We offer guided trips ranging from hourly rides out of our rustic lodge to ten-day excursions high into the Bridger Wilderness Area. There are no roads!

Trails wind through some of the most spectacular high mountain scenery in this country at around 10,000 feet elevation.

We pride ourselves in our fine horses and mules. We have a clean, professionally-staffed lodge and camp. Exclusive groups with four or more.

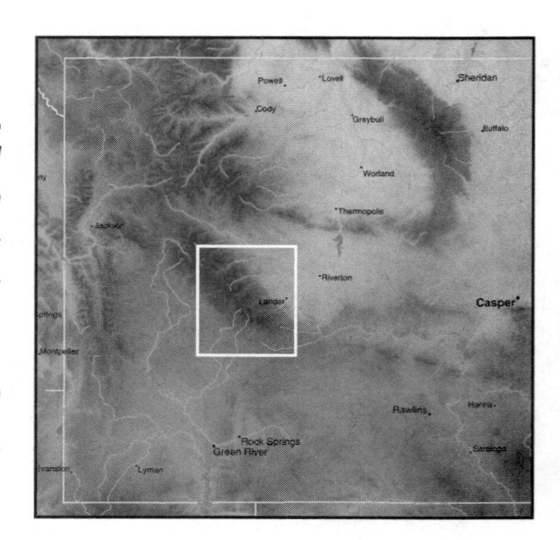

"The pleasant family atmosphere and delicious meals at this secluded ranch were delightful and the professional handling of our spot pack into the surrounding mountain was excellent!"
Cynthia Fisher

SEASONS OF OPERATION

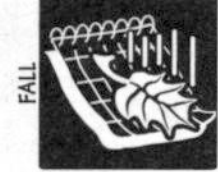

WESTERN ACTIVITIES

ACTIVITIES

SERVICES

BOULDER
LAKE
LODGE

Darby Mountain Outfitters

R. John Harper and Chuck Thornton
P.O. Box 447 • Big Piney, WY 83113
phone: R.John Harper (307) 276-3934 • Chuck Thornton (307) 386-9220

Pack trips are our specialty. From late June through September catch the fragrances of spring, see newborn wildlife, and enjoy colorful Indian autumns.

Our pack trips travel through an isolated mountain range in the center of the Wyoming Rockies, a place few people have seen.

Enjoy majestic scenery, fish mountain lakes for cutthroat and brook trout, and eat healthy western campfire meals under our big sky.

Experienced guides/packers will fit you to a horse and teach you how to ride in the mountains.

Just bring an adventuresome spirit and we will provide the rest!

"This experience is not for the faint of heart. Chuck Thornton offers a variety of mountain trips that caters to both the novice, as well as the most experienced horseman." Richard M. Saroney

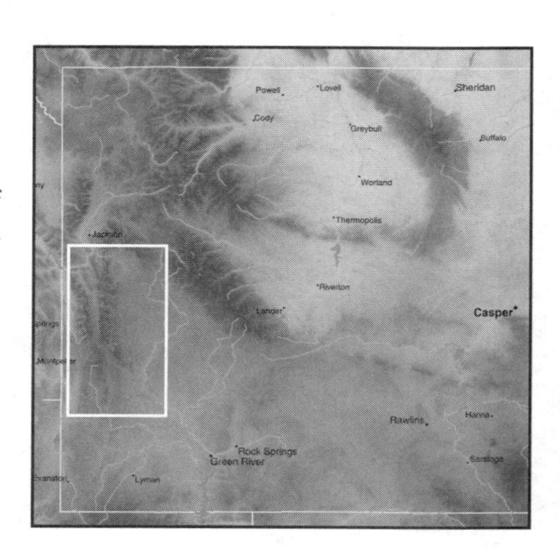

SEASONS OF OPERATION

WESTERN ACTIVITIES

ACTIVITIES

SERVICES

Big Piney, Wyoming

Darwin Ranch

Loring Woodman
P.O. Box 10430 • Jackson, WY 83002
phone: (307) 733-5588 • fax: (307) 739-0885

The Darwin Ranch has been catering to wilderness enthusiasts since 1965 when Loring Woodman began renovating the old log cabins which lay along the original, now obliterated, pioneer wagon track into Jackson Hole.

We are 22 miles inside Teton National Forest and have the last totally-isolated section of the Gros Ventre River to ourselves. Modern plumbing, electricity from Kinky Creek, a library, piano, and an accomplished, imaginative cook, complete the scene. Our maximum of 20 guests have a minimally-organized existence doing exactly what they want: riding, hiking, climbing, packtripping, and fly fishing.

The entire ranch, located 30 miles east of Jackson Hole, is available in winter for private gatherings of six to 12.

"Its location alone makes Darwin extraordinary because no other ranch has such isolated privacy and surroundings. Its isolation makes the logistic of providing its excellent services even more astonishing!" Mr. & Mrs. Craig Smythe

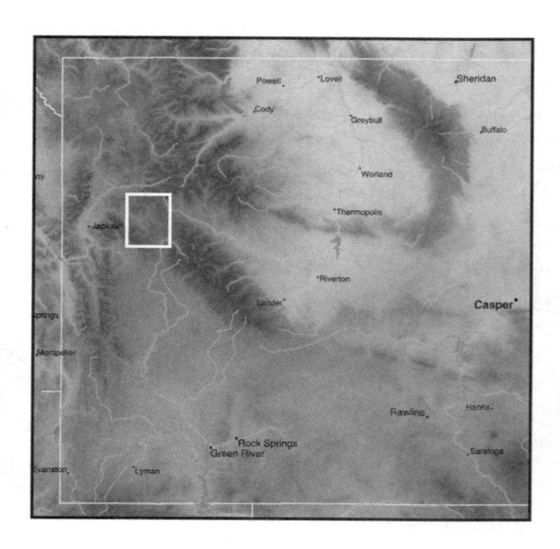

SEASONS OF OPERATION

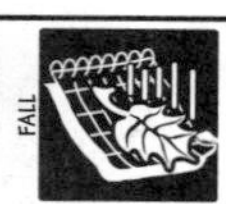

WESTERN ACTIVITIES

ACTIVITIES

SERVICES

Early Guest Ranch

Ruth and Wayne Campbell
7374 US Hwy. 26 • Crowheart, WY 82512 (summer)
phone: (307) 455-4055 (summer) • (314) 332-1234 • fax: (307) 455-2414
email: earlyranch@wyoming.com • www.earlyranch.com

Welcome, pardner. This is where you live the cowboy way. For one unforgettable week, the spirit of the West will invade your world. Leave your phones and stress behind and escape to a world of breathtaking skies and awe-inspiring Rocky Mountain scenery.

Horseback ride to your heart's content or just kick back and relax. Daily riding instructions leads the list of exciting ranch activities, which include self-guided river trips by canoe or raft, fly or rod fishing on the gorgeous Wind River, hiking, photography, knot-tying classes, square dancing and horseshoes, evening sing-along campfires, and stargazing. Kids love our "up and at 'em " Lil' Buckaroo program.

Our unique Sunrise Spa features aerobic classes, tanning, exercise machines and hot tub. The day's itinerary is tacked to your cabin door ... do as much or as little as you care to. Boy-howdy, ya tired yet?

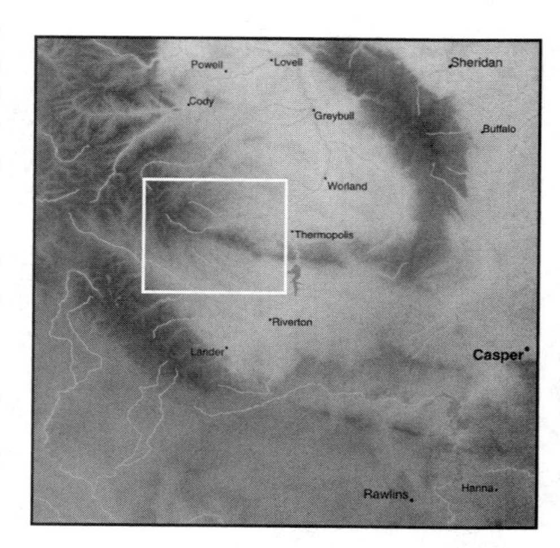

"Early Guest Ranch was truly a western experience!" Connie Hoffman

SEASONS OF OPERATION

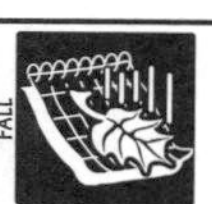

WESTERN ACTIVITIES

ACTIVITIES

SERVICES

EARLY
Guest Ranch
SALOON
BROKEN WHEEL BANK

John Henry Lee Outfitters, Inc.

John Lee
Box 8368 • Jackson, WY 83001
phone: (800) 352-2576 • (307) 733-9441 • fax: (307) 455-3215
email: infojhl@johnhenrylee.com • http://www.johnhenrylee.com

Travel by horseback into Yellowstone National Park or the Bridger Teton Wilderness.

Experience the spirit of adventure and exploration as you venture into a remote and secluded area for spectacular fishing and scenery. Photography and scenic trips move into the beautiful and breathtaking scenery of the high mountain country. There are abundant fields of wildflowers, lush alpine meadows, and lodgepole pine forests. This wilderness area offers you excellent opportunities to see a variety of wildlife in their natural habitat. You will enjoy the solitude and tranquil environment of the pristine wilderness. We maintain a clean and comfortable camp. All of our equipment and horses are in excellent shape. Our mountain-wise horses can accommodate even the most novice rider.

Hearty delicious meals are served by the campfire where the stories get better and better as the stars twinkle the night away.

"We can honestly say we enjoyed every minute of each trip and would highly recommend this outfitter to anyone who loves the outdoors, mountains, horses and adventures!" Jeani Smith

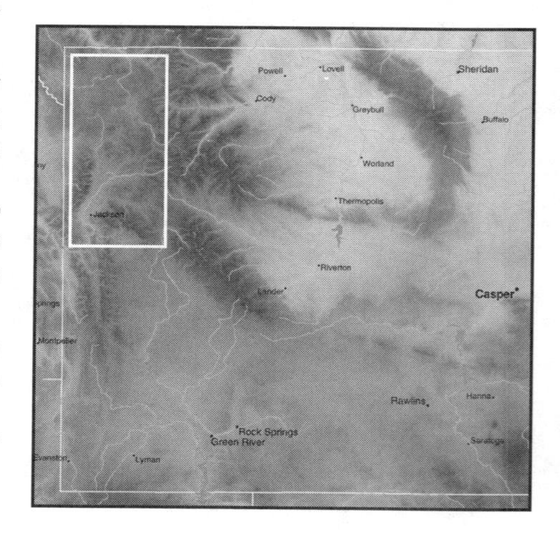

SEASONS OF OPERATION

WESTERN ACTIVITIES

ACTIVITIES

SERVICES

John Henry Lee
JHL
Outfitters, Inc.

K Bar Z Guest Ranch & Outfitters

Dave Segall and Dawna Barnett
P.O. Box 2167 • Cody, WY 82414
phone: (307) 587-4410 • fax: (307) 527-4605
www.agonline.com/KBarZ

K Bar Z Guest Ranch is nestled between the Beartooth and Absaroka mountain ranges, along the Chief Joseph Scenic Highway.

This guest ranch has everything you need to make your Wyoming vacation a trip to remember. Whether it is hiking a mountain trail, horseback riding through pristine meadows or fishing the famous Clarks Fork River for native cutthroat.

For the more adventurous, pack trips into the wilderness are available. Experienced guides and gentle horses will take you into the heart of the Rockies where you can see elk, deer, moose, mountain goat and even grizzly bear.

While at the ranch you will enjoy rustic cabins, family-style meals and good old western hospitality.

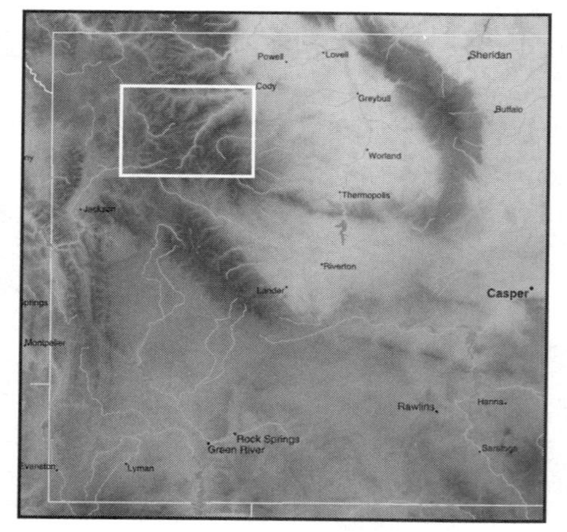

"This is an outstanding family operation!"
E.A. Karsgodt

SEASONS OF OPERATION

WESTERN ACTIVITIES

ACTIVITIES

SERVICES

Lozier's Box "R" Ranch

Levi M. Lozier

Box 100-PBYB • Cora, WY 82925
phone: (800) 822-8466 • (307) 367-4868 • fax: (307) 367-6260
email: boxr@wyoming.com • www.boxr.com

Experience the True West and Live that Life-Long Dream. Come join the Lozier's 100 year tradition on one of Wyoming's finest working cattle/horse guest ranches.

Nestled between two lakes, the Box "R" borders the Bridger National Forest, with 840,000 acres to ride and roam.

Ride from 7,500 to 11,000 feet elevation or move 25-1,000 head of cattle on our adults-only Lonesome Dove Cattle drives.

To ensure you of a top-notch riding vacation, the ranch has 100 head of finely trained horses/mules and boasts a 4-to-1 horse/guest ratio.

Unlimited riding with liberties and freedoms not found on other guest ranches.

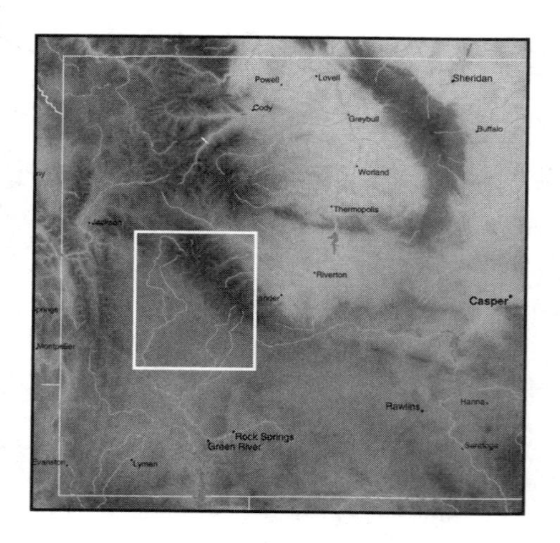

"The Lozier family is wonderful, warm, welcoming and a joy to 'reacquaint' with each year" Erin L. Burke

---

SEASONS OF OPERATION

WESTERN ACTIVITIES

ACTIVITIES

SERVICES

LOZIER'S
RANCH
CORA, WYOMING

Paintrock Adventures, L.L.C.

Todd Jones
P.O. Box 52 • Hyattville, WY 82428
phone: (307) 469-2274 • fax: (307) 469-2215
email: todd@paintrock.com • http://www.paintrock.com

Let us pack you into our wilderness camp of the world renowned Cloud Peak Wilderness. Stay at our base camp in above Grace Lake. Ride the trails of the Cheyenne, Shoshone, and Crow Indians in places called Tepee Pole Flats, Poacher Meadows and Solitude. Visit Kinky White's Trapper cabin and reminisce around the campfire about the outlaw Jake Johnson.

Our pack is very comfortable in a primitive kind of way, where you can relax and truly enjoy what this high country has to offer. We practice light on the land camping techniques with a definite western flavor.

Other activities include: hiking, fishing, searching for Indian artifacts and, of course, seeing a lot of wild country aboard your mountain-wise steed.

"I can imagine no one who does his job better with more honesty and integrity than this man (Todd Jones). One-of-a-kind outfitter providing one-of-a-kind adventures!" Lee Hofer, Eau Claire, WI

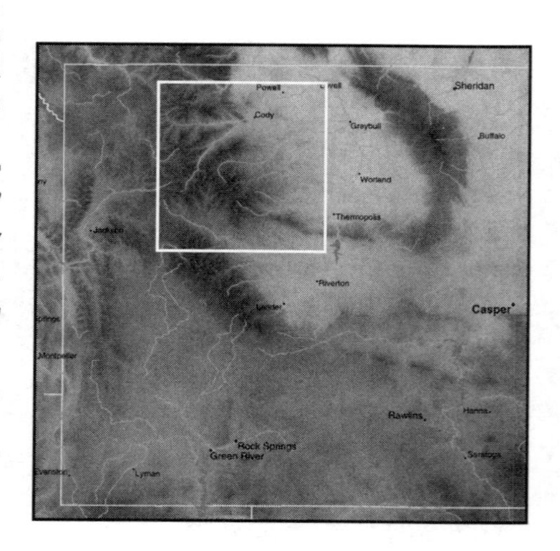

SEASONS OF OPERATION

WESTERN ACTIVITIES

ACTIVITIES

SERVICES

Triangle C Ranch

The Garnick Family
3737 U.S. Highway 26 • Dubois, WY 82513
phone: (307) 455-2225 • fax: (307) 455-2031

Triangle C Ranch where the Old West lives on. Located near Jackson Hole and Yellowstone National Park, the Triangle C Ranch hasn't changed much since the 1900's when the cowboys, tie hackers and mountain men roamed this Wind River Country. Sure, the old stage to Yellowstone is gone now, and there's a lot more modern conveniences, but its still run by honest, friendly, Wyoming folks. If you're looking for a life where the air is sweeter and the gallopin' years slow to a trot, we're playing your tune. We offer many activities and programs for old and young alike. Additionally, our guest's always look forward to the dinner bell calling them to the lodge's dining room.

We open our ranch gate and promise to send no one home without a fresh spring in their step and a treasured memory of cowboy'n on a ranch in the West.

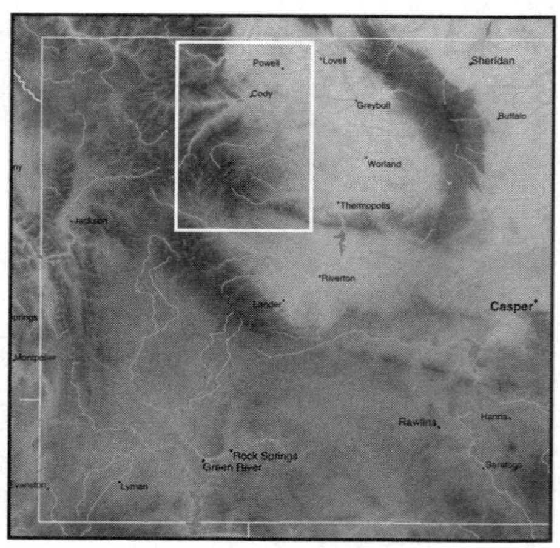

"Our trip to the Triangle C Ranch was a life-changing experience for the entire family. The scenery, location, amenities, and courteousness of the family/staff was unsurpassed in my lifetime!" Judy Karpis, Miami Springs, FL

SEASONS OF OPERATION

YEAR AROUND

Top Rated Professionals in
Canada

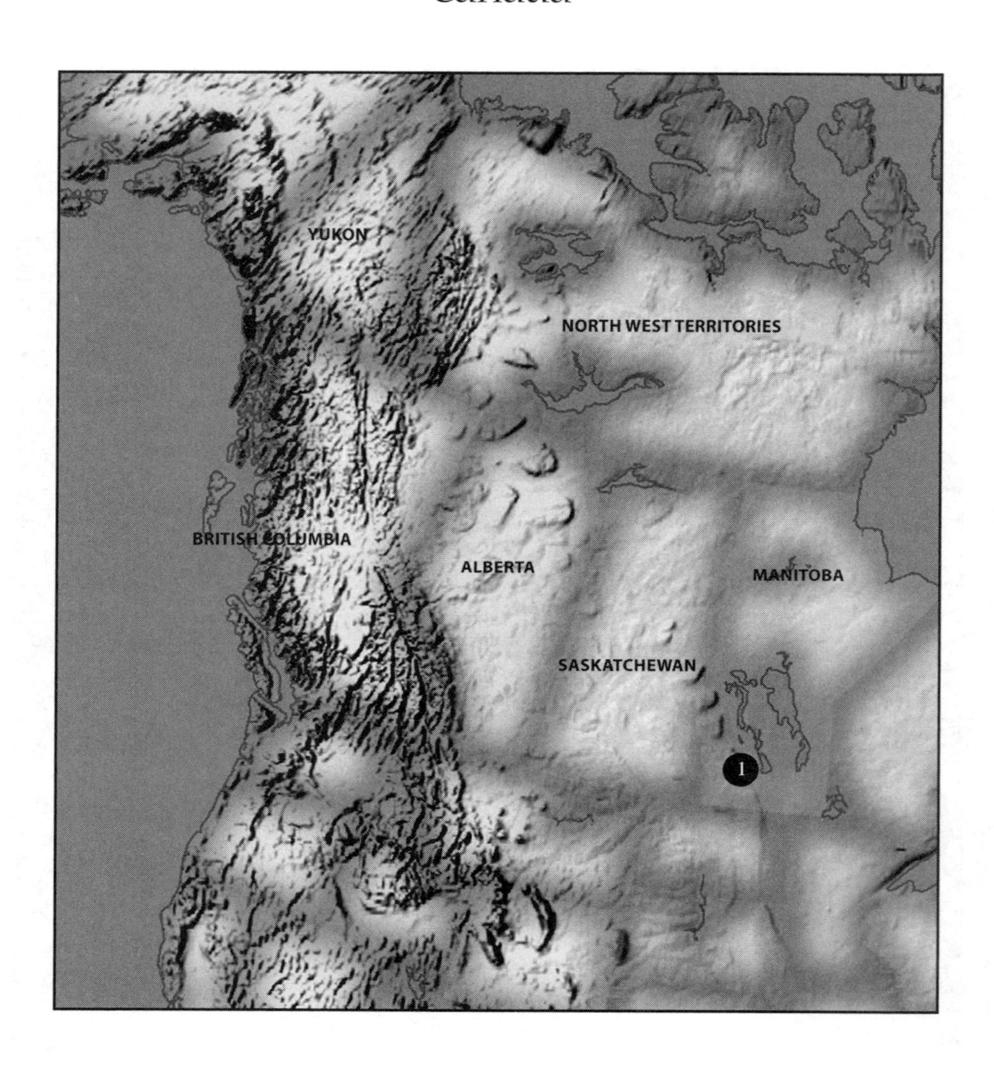

Outdoor Professionals

❶ Trailhead Ranch

Useful information for the province of

Manitoba

Ministries and Agencies

Department of Natural Resources
Legislative Building, Room 333
Winnipeg, MB Canada R3C 0V8
phone: (204) 945-3730

Dept. of Industry, Trade & Tourism
Travel Manitoba, Dept RH7
1515 Carlton St.
Winnipeg, MB Canada R3C 3H8
phone: (204) 945-3777/ext. RH7
fax: (204) 945-2302

Associations, Publications, etc.

DudeRanches.com
http://www.duderanches.com

Manitoba Lodges & Outfitters Assoc.
23 Sage Crescent
Winnipeg, MB Canada R2Y 0X8
phone: (204) 889-4840

License and Report Requirements

- All outfitters, guides and charter boats must be registered with each province.
- Business license needed to hunt or fish but does not require a year-end report.

Trailhead Ranch

Anne Schuster
Box 14 • Lake Audy, Manitoba, Canada R0J 0Z0
phone: (204) 848-7649

Trailhead means "the origin of pathways to adventure." Fittingly, exciting Canadian wilderness and family adventures have been all-season services at Trailhead Ranch since 1984. Private ranchhouse accommodations are situated near wildflower meadows and aspen forests, and are flanked by 3,000 square kilometers of rugged Riding Mountain National Park wilderness. Choose from day tours or overnight trips by covered wagon or on horseback. Hike, cycle or canoe the backcountry. At Trailhead, pioneering spirit is alive and well. "Cowboy-up!" Learn to ride, drive or pack a horse and throw a lasso. Try your hand at chuckwagon cooking. Track wildlife. Ranch owner and active host Anne Schuster provides genuine knowledge of Canada's pioneer heritage and its wilderness legacy.

Good horses, attentive hosts, and fascinating Canadian wilderness add up to great holiday adventure!

"A marvelous host! We were accommodated in every way possible in order to get maximum enjoyment from our stay."
Yude Henteloff

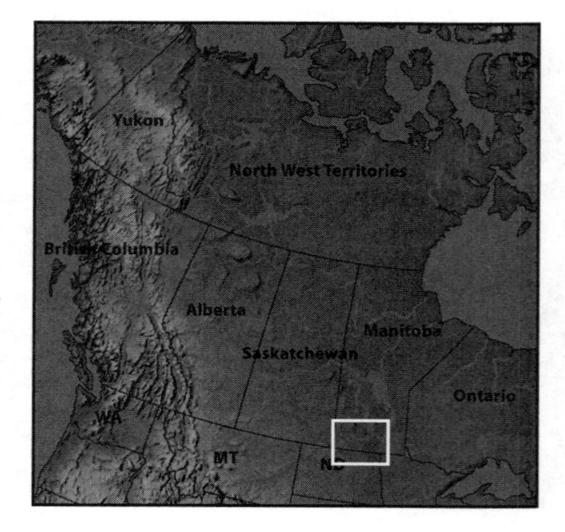

SEASONS OF OPERATION

YEAR AROUND

WESTERN ACTIVITIES

HORSEBACK

WAGON RIDES

HORSE PACK TRIPS

PACKING SCHOOL

COWBOY GAMES

BARREL RACING

BOOTS PROVIDED

ACTIVITIES

FLY FISHING

WILDLIFE VIEWING

ARCHEOLOGICAL SITES

HIKING/TREKKING

MOUNTAIN BIKING

GOLFING

SERVICES

CABINS

WALL TENTS

FAMILY

HANDICAP

FULL BOARD

DROP CAMPS

DAY TRIPS

GUIDED ACTIVITIES

TRAILHEAD RANCH

Appendix & Questionnaire & Indexes

Appendix - Western Adventures

This is a partial list of Pack Stations, Ranches Guides and Outfitters we contacted during the compilation of our book. Additional outdoor professionals and businesses were contacted during the compilation of all ten books in our Top Rated™ series, in all, during the compilation of the Top Rated™ concept, more than 23,000 professionals were contacted.

We invited them to participate in our survey by simply sending us their complete client list.

Some replied prizing our idea, but decided not to participate in our consumer guide books. Their main concern was the confidentiality of their client list. We truly respect this position, but we hope to have proven our honest and serious effort. We are sure they will join us in the next edition.

Others participated by sending their client list, but did not qualify for publication. In some cases because of a low score, and in other instances because of an insufficient number of questionnaires returned by their clients.

The names of the outdoor professionals who have qualified are **bolded** in the Appendix.

United States

Alabama

Company Blueridge Hunting Lodge
Contact John Robinson
City Lapine
Company Hamilton Hills Plantation, Inc.
Contact Lyle & Doug Smith
City Minter
Company Hawkins Ridge Lodge
Contact Hawkins Family
City Eufaula
Company Langford Farms Guided Hunts
Contact Peyton & Irene Langford
City Autaugaville
Company Macon County Guide Service
Contact Brian Thomas
City Shorter
Company Rockfence Stations
Contact Ray McClendon & Kane Hudmon
City Lafayette

Alaska

Company AAA Alaskan Outfitters Inc.
Contact Dan Schwarzer
City Anchorage
Company Adventure Alaska
Contact Todd Bureau
City Anchorage
Company Afishunt Charters
Contact John Baker
City Ninilchik
Company Air/Justin Tyme Guide Services
Contact Bill Woodin
City Soldotna
Company Alaska Bush Adventure
Contact Hugh Leslie Krank
City Anchorage
Company Alaska Guide Service - Master Guide
Contact Ken Fanning
City Yakutat
Company Alaska Outfitters
Contact Bill Stevenson
City Palmer
Company Alaska Remote Guide Service
Contact Wayne Kubat
City Wasilla
Company Alaska Ultima Thule Outfitters
Contact Paul & Donna Claus
City Anchorage
Company Alaskan Mountain Safaris
Contact Kenny Lake & Robert Fithian
City Copper Center
Company Angler's Choice Outdoor Adventures
Contact Richard Cameron
City Juneau
Company Artic North Guiding
Contact Dennis E. Reiner
City North Pole
Company Atkins Guiding & Flying Service-Master Guide
Contact Ray Atkins
City Cantwell
Company Beardown Adventures
Contact Neil Webster
City Eagle River
Company Bill Slemp's Wild Alaska
Contact William M. Slemp
City Soldotna
Company Black Fox Lodge
Contact Robert Wilkinson, Jr.
City Anchorage
Company Branham Adventures
Contact Dennis & Chris Branham
City Anchorage
Company Bristol Bay Outfitters
Contact John A. Peterson
City Anchorage
Company Brooks Range Adventures
Contact Arthur J. Andreis
City North Pole
Company Captain Cook Cruises
Contact Thomas A. Cook
City Auke Bay
Company D.Gunlogson Master Guide & Outfitter
Contact Dick Gunlogson
City Willow
Company Denali Wilderness Outfitters
Contact Kirk Martakis

City Cantwell
Company Eaglesong on Trail Lake
Contact Jennifer Kapla
City Eagle River
Company Grizzly Skins of Alaska
Contact Phil Shoemaker
City Wasilla
Company Happy Trails
Contact Andrew F. Paule
City Iliamna
Company Hautanen Enterprise
Contact Butch Hautanen
City Anchorage
Company J & R Enterprises
Contact Richard J. Ray
City Anchorage
Company Jacques Adventure Company
Contact Jerry Jacques
City Takleetna
Company Kichatna Guide Service - Master Guide
Contact Harold "Zeke" Schetzle
City Chugiak
Company Kitzen Guide Service
Contact Michael J. Litzen
City Kenai
Company Kniktuk Adventures
Contact Bob Wener
City Delta Junction
Company Kobuk Guide and Outfitters
Contact Henry C. Clark
City Solodtna
Company Kodiak Safaris
Contact Steven Perins & Buckey Windley
City Anchorage
Company Lake Country Lodge, Inc.
Contact John C. Davis
City Soldotna
Company LaRose Guide Service - Master Guide
Contact Gary LaRose
City Anchorage
Company Larry Rivers Master Guide & Outfitter
Contact Larry R. & Naomi Rivers
City Talkeetna
Company Last Frontier Guiding & Outfitting-Master Guide
Contact Rocky Keen
City Palmer
Company Lost Creek Ranch
Contact Les and Norma Cobb
City Fairbanks
Company Mark's Guide Service - Master Guide
Contact Mark Sandland
City Anchorage
Company Midnight Sun Adventures - Master Guide
Contact Philip Driver
City Anchorage
Company Midnight Sun Wilderness Safaris
Contact Coke W. Wallace
City Healy
Company Morris Hunting Company
Contact Steven Morris
City Anchorage
Company Mulchatna Lodge
Contact
City Palmer
Company Mystic Lake Lodge - Master Guide
Contact George Palmer
City Palmer
Company Nin Ridge Guides
Contact Karl G. Braendel
City Chickaloon
Company Osprey Island Lodge
Contact Gary C. Pogany
City Eagle River
Company Panorama Mountain Outfitters
Contact R. L. "Butch" Loper
City Talkeetna
Company Parker/Boyce Guide Service, Inc.
Contact Bruce Parker & James Boyce
City Sitka
Company Pioneer Outfitters - Master Guide
Contact Terry L. Overly
City Chisana
Company R & R Guide Service
Contact Rod Schuh & Rob Jones
City Anchorage
Company RiteOFF
Contact President Michael D. Justice
City Anchorage
Company Rob Holt Registered Guide/ Outfitter
Contact Robert N. Holt
City Talkeetna
Company Rogue Charters/Beacon Hill Lodge
Contact Cynthia & Ronald Moyer
City Ketchikan
Company See Alaska - Master Guide
Contact Jim H. Keeline
City Juneau
Company Sheep River Hunting Camps
Contact Ed and Deb Stevenson
City Wasilla
Company Silver Bullet Kenai River Guide Service
Contact John F. Joseph
City Anchorage
Company Spiridon Camp - Master Guide
Contact Leon J. Francisco
City Kodiak
Company Stephan Lake Ldg & Kodiak Guides-Master Guide
Contact Jim Bailey
City Eagle River
Company Stoney River Lodge
Contact Mark "Curly" J. Warren
City Chugiak
Company T.C. Lewis Lodge
Contact Joe & Candie Caraway
City Beluga
Company Tom Hundley Master Guide & Outfitter
Contact Tom Hundley
City Palmer
Company Tracy Vrem's Blue Mountain Lodge
Contact Tracy J. Vrem
City Chugiak
Company Tsiu River Lodge
Contact Samuel T. Fejes, Jr.
City Anchorage
Company Upriver Outfitters
Contact Rick Sylvester
City Dillingham
Company VanNest's Alaskan Wildlife Photo
Contact Timothy J. VanNest Jr.
City Palmer
Company Wildman Lake Lodge
Contact Gary "Butch" King Jr.
City Anchorage
Company Wildman Lake Lodge - Master Guide
Contact Keith N. Johnson
City Anchorage
Company Wolf Creek Outfitters
Contact Thomas W. Hillis
City Fairbanks
Company Wrangell R. Ranch - Master Guide
Contact Ray McNutt
City Anchorage

Arizona

Company Arizona Outfitters
Contact Milton and Pete Davis
City Forest Lakes
Company Black River Guide & Outfitting
Contact Steve Clonts
City Eagar
Company Brush Busters Trophy Hunts
Contact Scott Brush
City Mesa
Company Chaparral Guides & Outfitters
Contact Bill Marshall
City Payson
Company Circle Z Ranch
Contact
City Patagonia
Company Dorulla Outfitters
Contact Ronald N. Dorulla
City Flagstaff
Company Double J Outfitters
Contact Jim & Jenny Heap
City St. Johns
Company Elkhorn Ranch
Contact
City Tucson
Company Fir Mountain Ranch Outfitters, Inc.
Contact Franz & Maria Brun
City Tucson
Company Grapevine Canyon Guest Ranch
Contact Eve & Gerry Searle
City Pearce
Company Honeymoon Trail Company
Contact
City Moccasin
Company Hualapai Wildlife Conservation
Contact Monroe Beecher

City Peach Springs
Company JFK Guide and Outfitter
Contact Kip Fattaleh
City Phoenix
Company Kay El Bar Ranch
Contact Jane Nash
City Wickenburg
Company King Guide Service
Contact Dan & Monica King
City Tucson
Company Lazy K Bar Ranch
Contact William Scott & Carol Moore
City Tucson
Company Maynard Ranch
Contact Perry & Brenda Hunsaker and Billy & Nora Maynard
City Higley
Company Mogollon Rim Outfitters & Guides
Contact Gregory M. Krogh
City Cornville
Company Nichols Guiding Service
Contact Jared Nichols
City Gilbert
Company Ponderosa Outfitters & Guide Service
Contact Ron Eichelberger
City Peoria
Company Pusch Ridge Outfitters
Contact Dale & Roxanne Kelso
City Oro Valley
Company Ram Riders Guides & Outfitters
Contact Michael Mell
City Show Low
Company Rincon Outfitters
Contact Robert M. Dryden
City Tucson
Company Rough Country Outfitters
Contact Wayne K. Curtis
City Thatcher
Company San Carlos Apache Tribe
Contact
City San Carlos
Company Sheep Ltd.
Contact Larry Heathington
City Kingman
Company Sonora Outfitters
Contact Leon Hoeffer
City Nogales
Company Tanque Verde Ranch
Contact
City Tucson
Company Timberline Outfitters
Contact James (Perry) & Brenda Hunsaker
City Higley
Company Trophy Outfitters/US Outfitters/Cougar Unltd.
Contact Van D. Hale
City Eagar
Company Weminuche Wilderness Adventures
Contact Dan Shupe
City Apache Junction
Company Yellowhorn Outfitters/Sand Tank Outfitters
Contact Peter A. Cimellaro
City Phoenix

Arkansas

Company Beaver Creek Outfitters II
Contact Lawrence D. Arnold
City Wiseman
Company Cache River Outfitters
Contact Bert & Cheryl Haralson
City Augusta
Company Hunting & Fishing World, Inc.
Contact Willima Elder
City Bull Shoals
Company Scott Valley Resort & Guest Ranch
Contact Tom & Kathleen Cooper
City Mountain Home

California

Company Arrow Five Outfitters
Contact Jim Schaafsma
City Zenia
Company Bigfoot Mountaineering
Contact
City Bakersfield
Company Coffee Creek Ranch
Contact Ruth Hartman
City Trinity Center
Company Jerry Penland Guide Service
Contact Jerry Penland
City Palo Cedro
Company Kennedy Meadows Resort & Pack
Contact
City Sonora
Company Prophet Muskwa Outfitters
Contact Kevin & Victoria Olmstead
City Friant
Company River S Enterprises
Contact Mike & Debbie Schwiebert
City Santa Margarita
Company Slack's Wilderness Adventures
Contact Mark Slack
City Eureka
Company Spanish Springs Ranch
Contact Barbara Roberts
City Ravendale
Company Tom Willoughby Outfitter/ Guide Service
Contact Thomas Charles Willoughby
City King City
Company Triangle C Outfitters
Contact Bruce Cahill
City Riverside

Colorado

Company 4 + 2 T Ranch
Contact Craig T. Tomke
City Hayden
Company 7-M Guide Service
Contact Seven Mazzone
City Durango
Company Action Adventures
Contact
City Montrose
Company Adams Lodge
Contact Ron Hilkey
City Meeker
Company Al's Outfitting
Contact Allen J. Roberts
City Montrose
Company Alexander Outfitters
Contact Dave & Kerry Alexander
City Norwood
Company All Seasons Ranch
Contact M. Bruce Cottrell
City Colorado Springs
Company Anderson's Guide Service
Contact Daniel J. Anderson
City Del Norte
Company Aspen Canyon Ranch
Contact David Lewis & Steven Roderick
City Parshall
Company Astraddle A Saddle Inc.
Contact Gary Bramwell
City Pagosa Springs
Company Avalanche Outfitters
Contact Mike Schilling
City Carbondale
Company B 4 J Outfitters
Contact Robert Jeffreys Jr.
City New Castle
Company Backcountry Outfitters
Contact Bill Yeagher
City Steamboat Springs
Company Backcountry Outfitters, Inc.
Contact David & Nancy Guilliams
City Pagosa Springs
Company Badger Basin Outfitters
Contact Randy E. Tinlge
City Fairplay
Company Badger Creek Guide & Outfitter
Contact Tim R. Hamilton
City Hamilton
Company Basin Outfitters
Contact Kenneth E. Wissel
City Loma
Company Bear Basin Ranch
Contact Gary Ziegler
City Westcliffe
Company Bearcat Outfitters
Contact Seth Peters
City Craig
Company Beaver Meadows Resort Ranch
Contact Don & Linda Weixelman
City Red Feather Lakes
Company Beaver Mountain Outfitters
Contact Duain Morton
City Dolores
Company Beaver Valley Ranch

Contact Michael Cosby
City Englewood
Company Big Cimarron Outfitters
Contact Matt or Ken Munyon
City Olathe
Company Big Creek Reserve
Contact John E. Sandelin
City Steamboat Springs
Company Big Mountain Outfitters
Contact Sam Potter
City Rifle
Company Big Timbers Guest Ranch Inc.
Contact Brad Nothnagel & Dean Wagner
City Littleton
Company Bill Law Guide Service
Contact Bill Law
City Mesa
Company Black Elk Guides & Outfitters
Contact
City Carbondale
Company Black Mesa Lodge
Contact Tom McLeod
City Delta
Company Black Timber Outfitters
Contact Kent Fischer & Carroll Johnson
City Cedaredge
Company Blanco River Outfitters
Contact Carl Bentley
City Pagosa Springs
Company Blays Western Colorado Outfitters
Contact Gordon Blay
City Montrose
Company Blue Creek Outfitters
Contact Scott Dillon
City Naturita
Company Bookcliff Outfitters
Contact Bruce Nay
City Norwood
Company Breckenridge Outfitters Inc.
Contact Paul H. Brooks
City Breckenridge
Company Broadacres Guest Ranch
Contact
City Creede
Company Broken Spoke Ranch
Contact Clifford Davis
City Whitewater
Company Brush Creek Outfitters Inc.
Contact Dennis Russell Grieve
City Snowmass Village
Company Buck Ridge Outfitters
Contact Ed Ilhareguy
City Loma
Company Buck's Livery Inc.
Contact Ben & Mindy Breed
City Durango
Company Bud Flowers Guide & Outfitters
Contact Bud Flowers
City Montrose
Company Bull Basin Guides & Outfitters
Contact Dean Billington
City Arvada
Company Bull's Eye Outfitters Inc.
Contact Warren R. Allmon
City Basalt
Company Burton's Guide Service
Contact Clyde Warren Bruton
City Mesa
Company C & M Outfitters
Contact Marcus Walker
City Fairplay
Company Cache Creek Outfitters
Contact Jim DeKam
City Parachute
Company Cadwell Outfitters
Contact Curtis Cadwell
City Powderhorn
Company Calhoun Guide & Outfitting
Contact Jay Jefferson & Bob Stokes
City Grand Junction
Company Camilletti and Son's Inc.
Contact Edward Camilletti
City Milner
Company Canyon Creek Outfitter
Contact Frank Fraser
City New Castle
Company Capitol Peak Outfitters
Contact Steve & Sandy Rieser
City Carbondale
Company Chair Mountain Stables
Contact Tom Mainer III
City Redstone
Company Challenge Outfitters
Contact David Eider
City Steamboat Springs
Company Champion Outfitters
Contact Dale V. Sundblom
City Bayfield
Company Chaparral Park General Store
Contact Karen Johnston
City Hartsel
Company Cherokee Outfitters
Contact Chuck Baker
City Meeker
Company Cherokee Park Ranch
Contact
City Livermore
Company Chris Loncarich Guide Service
Contact Chris Loncarich
City Fruita
Company Circle Bar Outfitting
Contact Larry Allen
City Hotchkiss
Company Circle K Ranch , Inc.
Contact Al & Joan Cannon/Cindy Beecher
City Dolores
Company Cirrus Corporation
Contact Gary White
City Denver
Company Coal Basin Partners
Contact
City Ridgway
Company Coal Creek Outfitting
Contact Rod Black
City Gunnison
Company Colorado Back Country Outfitters
Contact Alan Bishop
City Montrose
Company Colorado Guest Ranch
Contact Larry & Elaine Mautz
City Paonia
Company Colorado High Country Outfitters
Contact Steven Weaver
City Phippsburg
Company Colorado High County Outfitters
Contact The Hatlees
City Phippsburg
Company Colorado High Guide Service
Contact Dennis Bergstad & Cade Benson
City Parker
Company Colorado Trail Riders & Outfitters
Contact Doug Flowers
City Montrose
Company Colorado Trails Ranch
Contact
City Durango
Company Colorado's Mountain West Outfitting Co.
Contact WIlly Pete Georgiou
City Craig
Company Columbine Outfitters
Contact Dan Bell
City Frisco
Company Conejos River Outfitters
Contact Walter Heady Jr.
City Alamosa
Company Cooper's Outfitting & Guide Service
Contact Paul Cooper & Mark Chiono
City Grand Junction
Company Coulter Lake Guest Ranch Inc.
Contact C. Norman Benzinger
City Rifle
Company Cowboy Camp Outfitters Inc.
Contact Robert Port
City Arvada
Company Culbreath Cattle Co.
Contact Grady Culbreath
City Kremmling
Company D & G Horses
Contact Dale Coombs
City Rifle
Company Dan Hughes Outfitting & Guides
Contact Dan Hughes
City Parlin
Company Dave Yost Outfittters
Contact Merrilee Yost
City Walden
Company Devils Thumb Ranch Resort Inc.
Contact Barry John Gordon
City Tabernash
Company Diamond D Bar Ranch
Contact Obbie & Willa Lee Dickey
City Del Norte
Company Diamond Hitch Stables & Outfitting
Contact Joe Fahrion
City Pagosa Springs
Company Diamond M Outfitters
Contact Bob Martin
City Pagosa Springs
Company Diamond S Ranch
Contact Mike Walck
City Eagle

Company Dilley's Guide Service
Contact Dale Dilley
City South Fork
Company Dog Gone Outfitters
Contact Perry Williamson
City Slater
Company Double B Ranch Outfitters Inc.
Contact William D. Harmon
City Basalt
Company DTD Outfitters
Contact Jack Lowe
City Delta
Company Eagle Spirit Outfitters
Contact Carl Spina
City Loveland
Company Eagle's Nest Outfitting
Contact Billy Howard
City Meeker
Company East Divide Outfitters Inc.
Contact Dennis Yost
City Glenwood Springs
Company Echo Canyon Guest Ranch
Contact David Hampton
City La Veta
Company Elite Outfitters
Contact Brian Newell
City Denver
Company Elk County Outfitters
Contact David Butterfield
City Montrose
Company Elk Mountain Guides & Outfitter
Contact John Pickering
City New Castle
Company Elk Mountain Ranch
Contact
City Buena Vista
Company Elk Ridge Adventures
Contact Stephen F. Watwood
City Oak Creek
Company Elk River Guest Ranch
Contact Patrick Barrett & William Hinder
City Clark
Company Elkhorn Outfitters Inc.
Contact Richard & Cheryl Dodds
City Craig
Company Elkstream Outfitters Inc.
Contact Jon T. Van Ingen
City Glenwood Springs
Company Engine Creek Outfitters
Contact Jim Houghton
City Durango
Company Farris Outfitters
Contact Paul Farris
City Black Forest
Company Fawn Gulch Outfitters
Contact Dave Hemauer
City Pagosa Springs
Company Finlay River Outfitters
Contact
City Glenwood Springs
Company Flyfisher Guide Service
Contact Reynolds G. Cannon
City Denver
Company Flynn & Sons Outfitters
Contact Delnor Flynn
City Crawford
Company Fossil Ridge Guide Service
Contact Rudy & Deb Rudibaugh
City Parlin
Company Fox Creek Adventures Inc.
Contact Cal Junker
City Antonito
Company Frazier Outfitting
Contact Sammy Frazier
City Creede
Company Fritzlan's Guest Ranch
Contact Calvin Fritzlan Outfitter
City Meeker
Company Garvey Bros. Outfitters
Contact Doylene & Stan Garvey
City Nucla
Company Geneva Park Outfitters
Contact Terry Sandmeier
City Conifer
Company Gerald Field Outfitters
Contact Gerald Field
City Montrose
Company Gorsuch Outfitters
Contact Scott Gorsuch
City Vail
Company Granite Mountain Lodge Inc.
Contact Susan Glittenberg
City Sargents
Company Great Divide Outfitters
Contact Dan Newman
City Bayfield
Company Green Acres Ranch
Contact Terry Green
City Oak Creek
Company H & H Hunting Camp Inc.
Contact
City Grand Lake
Company Hammer Packing & Meat Processing
Contact James Hammer
City Yampa
Company Hanging Horse Ranch Outfitter
Contact Colby Olford
City Collbran
Company Hawk Creek Outfitting Co.
Contact Wesley T. Gore
City Rifle
Company Hermosa Creek Outfitters
Contact Frank Morningstar
City Durango
Company High Country Guide & Outfitter
Contact Paul Irwin
City Craig
Company High Meadow Outfitters
Contact
City Bayfield
Company High Plains Outfitters
Contact Donny E. Talton II
City Pueblo
Company High Plateau Outfitters Ltd.
Contact Angela Vannucci
City Larkspur
Company High Trail Outfitters Inc.
Contact Bill Hopp
City Avon
Company High West Outfitters
Contact Robert Knowlton & Kim Miller
City Sanford
Company Highlands Unlimited Inc.
Contact Geoff Burby
City Hesperus
Company Hill's Guide Service
Contact Clifford & Jancice Hill
City Colbran
Company Hillview Outfitters
Contact Willard Forman
City Morrison
Company Holman's High Country Outfitters
Contact Buddy Holman
City Montrose
Company Honaker Guides & Packers
Contact Pat Honaker
City Yellow Jacket
Company Horn Fork Guides
Contact Joe Boucher
City Towner
Company Horsethief Adventures
Contact
City DeBeque
Company Hoza Guide & Outfitting
Contact Tony Hoza
City Norwood
Company Hyatt Guides & Outfitters
Contact Bruce Hyatt
City Montrose
Company Imperial Expeditions
Contact Micheal John Jones
City Pueblo
Company J & B Outfitters
Contact Brad Gray
City Montrose
Company J & J Guides & Outfitters
Contact John Markham
City Nederland
Company J M L Outfitters
Contact Maggie & Marie Haskett
City Englewood
Company Jackson's Guide & Outfitter Service
Contact Robert Jackson
City Denver
Company Jeffcoat Outfitters
Contact Danny Jeffcoat
City Hamilton
Company Jerry Craig Guide Service
Contact Jerry Craig
City Granby
Company K & W Outifitters
Contact Drew & Billie Kissire
City Crawford
Company Keystone Resort
Contact Phillip Stahl
City Keystone
Company Kuhns' Guide & Outfitters
Contact Douglas Kuhns
City Lamar
Company Lake Mancos Ranch
Contact
City Mancos
Company Lakeview Resort & Outfitters
Contact Dan & Michelle Murphy
City Lake City
Company Lakota Guides & Outfitters
Contact Bob Littlejohn
City Paonia

Company Lamicq Guides & Outfitters Inc
Contact John & Diane Lamicq
City Grand Junction
Company Little Cone Outfitters
Contact Roy Hutt
City Norwood
Company Little Creek Ranch
Contact Alan Baier
City Collbran
Company Little Grizzly Creek Ranch Inc.
Contact Leo Douglas Sysel
City Walden
Company Lobo Outfitters
Contact Dick Ray & Mike Ray
City Pagosa Springs
Company Lodgepole Outfitters
Contact Don Pinnt
City Grand Junction
Company Lone Tom Outfitting
Contact Paul Janke
City Meeker
Company Lost Creek Guides
Contact Lance Edinger
City Meeker
Company M & M Outfitters
Contact Tom and Susan Mikesell
City Craig
Company Mad Adventures, Inc.
Contact Roger Hedlund
City Winter Park
Company Mamm Peak Outfitters
Contact Jeff & Dea Mead
City Grand Junction
Company Marvine Ranch LLC & Elk Creek Lodge
Contact William Wheeler
City Meeker
Company McCombs Hunting Camp, Inc.
Contact Susan M. Phillips
City Lewis
Company Meadows Vega
Contact Tom Cox
City Colbran
Company Mike Murphy Wilderness Exp.
Contact
City Durango
Company Mill Creek Outfitters
Contact Chuck Wisecup
City Oak Creek
Company Mineral Mountain Guide & Outfitters
Contact John Martin
City Powderhorn
Company Mule Creek Outfitters
Contact Randy & Brenda Myers
City Lake George
Company Mule Shoe Guide Servie
Contact Billy Joe Dilley
City Monte Vista
Company Natural Adventures Inc.
Contact Thomas E. Tietz
City Littleton
Company Needle Rock Ranch
Contact Steven Duffy
City Crawford
Company Noah's Ark Adventure Program Ltd
Contact Chuck Cichowitz
City Buena Vista
Company North Fork Ranch
Contact
City Shawnee
Company North Park Outfitters
Contact Bob Martin
City Steamboat Springs
Company OFC Outfitting
Contact
City Gypsum
Company OK Ranch Outfitters
Contact John Carelli
City Whitewater
Company Old West Outfitters
Contact Randy Messick
City Buena Vista
Company Pack Country Outfitters
Contact Mike Reid
City Vail
Company Peaceful Valley Lodge & Guest Ranch
Contact
City Lyons
Company Peters Hunting Service
Contact Harley & Bonnie
City Rangely
Company Piedra Packing & Outfitting
Contact Roger Kleckner
City Pagosa Springs
Company Platte River Outfitters
Contact Richard Aldrich
City Littleton
Company Pomotawh Naantam Ranch
Contact Jon & Dori Lee
City Somerset
Company Powderhorn Guest Ranch
Contact Jim & Bonnie Cook
City Powderhorn
Company Prime Time Hunts
Contact William Malizia
City Loveland
Company Proline Excursions Inc.
Contact Paul Howard
City Wheat Ridge
Company Ram's Horn Guides & Outfitters
Contact Alan Vallejo
City Woodland Park
Company Red Feather Guides & Outfitters
Contact Todd Peterson
City Vail
Company Rendezvous Outfitters & Guides
Contact Russ & Cheri Eby
City Gunnison
Company Rimrock Guide & Outfitting
Contact Charles Harrington
City Cedaridge
Company Ripple Creek Lodge
Contact Ken Jett
City Denver
Company Rock Creek Outfitters
Contact Robert E. Thompson
City Rand
Company Rocky Mountain Outfitters
Contact Colt Ross
City Bayfield
Company Rocky Mountain Safaris
Contact Denzel Hartshorn
City Grand Juction
Company Rocky Pappas Guides & Outfitters
Contact
City Clifton
Company Saddle Action
Contact Pam Green
City Edwards
Company Samuelson Outfitters
Contact Dick & Cathy Samuelson
City Fraser
Company San Juan Outfitting
Contact Tom & Cheri Van Soelen
City Durango
Company San Pahgre Outdoor Adventures
Contact Stuart Chappell
City Montrose
Company Sangre De Cristo Outfitters
Contact Tom & Bill Schulze
City Westcliffe
Company Schmittel Packing & Outfitting
Contact David & Verna Schmittel
City Saguache
Company Scoop Lake Outfitters Ltd.
Contact David Suitts
City Boulder
Company Scott Fly Rod Co.
Contact John Duncan
City Telluride
Company Sky Corral Guest Ranch
Contact David Vannice
City Bellvue
Company Skyline Guest Ranch
Contact Mike and Sheila Farny
City Telluride
Company Sly Creek Guide & Outfitters
Contact Gary Baysinger
City Craig
Company Snowmass Falls Outfitters
Contact Mat Turnbull
City Snowmass Village
Company Snowmass Stables Inc.
Contact Marlene Christopher
City Snowmass Village
Company Solomon Creek Outfitter
Contact Nancy Solomon
City Oak Creek
Company Southwest Adventures Ltd.
Contact Charles Hughes
City Redvale
Company Spadafora Ranches Lodge
Contact Roger Cesario
City Crested Butte
Company Sperry's
Contact Joe Sperry
City Delta
Company Spike's Outfitters
Contact Perry Alspaugh
City Del Norte
Company Steamboat Stables/Sombrero Ranches Inc.
Contact Rex Walker
City Boulder

Company Stetson Ranches LLC
Contact Franklin L. Stetson
City Maybell
Company Sunrise Outfitters
Contact Leroy & Paul Schroeder
City Rifle
Company T Lazy 7 Ranch
Contact Rick Deane
City Aspen
Company Taylor Creek Inc.
Contact William Fitzsimmons
City Basalt
Company Taylor Guide & Outfitters
Contact Lance & Terri Taylor
City Arboles
Company Teocalli Outfitters
Contact Al & Laura Van Dyke
City Crested Butte
Company The Don K Ranch
Contact
City Pueblo
Company The Home Ranch
Contact Ken & Cile Jones
City Clark
Company Thompson's High County Guides & Outfitters
Contact Greg Thompson
City Breckenridge
Company Three String Outfitting & Guiding
Contact Dennis Clendenning
City Fort Collins
Company Timber Basin Outfitters
Contact Gregory Geelhoed
City Grand Juction
Company Timberline Outfitters
Contact Douglas Frank Jr.
City Lake City
Company Triple G Outfitter & Guides Inc.
Contact Daniel Eckert & Alan Echtler
City Wolcott
Company Triple-O-Outfitters
Contact Larry & Reta Osborn
City Hamilton
Company Two Rivers Guest Ranch
Contact
City Meeker
Company Ute Trail Guide Service
Contact Glenn Everett
City Salida
Company W3 Outfitters
Contact Dale & Sheri Hopwood
City Fruita
Company Walz Guide Service
Contact Jimmie Walz Sr.
City Grand Junction
Company Watkins San Juan Outfitting
Contact Thomas F. Watkins
City Ridgeway
Company Waunita Hot Springs Ranch
Contact Ryan Pringle
City Gunnison
Company Welder Outfitting Service
Contact Brian & Shawn Welder
City Meeker
Company West Elk Outfitters
Contact John Hatlem
City Crested Butte
Company Western Horizon's Guides & Outfitters
Contact Myron Morrow
City Bailey
Company Western Sports
Contact Robert O. Woods
City Basalt
Company Western Ways Ltd.
Contact Eric Glade
City Lakewood
Company Western Wildlife Inc.
Contact Rob Raley
City Meeker
Company White Pine Ranch
Contact Dennis & Cindy Hall
City Gunnison
Company White River Resort
Contact Jack Harrison
City Aurora
Company Wild West Outfitters
Contact Allen Kennon
City Montrose
Company Wilderness Adventures Inc.
Contact Larry Ehardt
City South Fork
Company Wilderness West
Contact Gordon Kent & Scott Garber
City Pagosa Springs
Company Willow Creek Outfitters
Contact Don Hawkins
City Delta
Company Winding Stair Mountain Outfitters
Contact Sam Smith
City La Jara
Company Yampa Valley Outfitters LLC
Contact Mack & Boyd Tallent
City Craig

Florida

Company Allen Duke
Contact
City Port St. Joe
Company Cowboys Charter, Inc.
Contact Mr. Baumgarten
City Key West
Company Daniel S. Andrews
Contact
City Cape Canaveral
Company Eagle's Nest Hunt Club Inc.
Contact
City Orlando
Company George Montesino
Contact
City Captiva
Company John M. Prybil
Contact
City Islamorada
Company John W. Manning, III
Contact Midland Michigan Mel Su Jac
City Key Largo
Company Roy C. String, Jr.
Contact
City Sarasota
Company Steven L. Westervelt
Contact
City Naples
Company Terry C. Middleton
Contact
City Ft. Myers
Company Trek International Safaris
Contact Mike Cloaninger
City Ponte Vedra Beach
Company William H. Trimble, Jr.
Contact
City Bokeelia

Idaho

Company 4 x 4 Outfitters, Inc
Contact Gary Madsen
City Ellis
Company American Adrenaline Company, Inc.
Contact Deb Wood & Steven E. Zettel
City Challis
Company Artic Creek Lodge
Contact Jack P. Smith
City North Fork
Company B & K Outfitters
Contact Brian E. Butz
City Sandpoint
Company B Bar C Outfitters
Contact Mike & Belinda Stockton
City Orofino
Company Barker Trophy Hunts
Contact Jon Barker
City Lewiston
Company Bear Creek Outfitters
Contact Lyle Phelps
City Weippe
Company Bear River Outfitters
Contact Marriner R. Jensen
City Montpelier
Company Big Track Outfitters
Contact Johannsen & Johannsen
City Gooding
Company Bigfoot Outfitters
Contact Harvey Whitten & Tom Fliss
City Riggins
Company Bighorn Outfitters
Contact George Butcher & Dave Melton
City Carmen
Company Birch Creek & Clearwater Driftr.
Contact David L. Peterson
City Orofino
Company Boulder Creek Outfitters Inc.
Contact Tim Craig & Allen D. Jones
City Peck
Company C Bar D Outfitters
Contact Darrell Meddle
City Kamiah
Company Cat Track Outfitters
Contact Todd Molitor
City Jerome
Company Central Idaho Outfitters
Contact Stephen A. Kaschmitter
City Grangeville

Company Chamberlain Basin Outfitters, Inc.
Contact Tony & Tracy Krekeler
City Salmon
Company Chuckar Chasers
Contact Rick Schultsmeier
City Boise
Company Clearwater Outfitters
Contact Thomas J. Rucker
City Weippe
Company Coeur D'Alene River Big Game Outfitters
Contact Gary & Jan Sylte
City Athol
Company Diamond D Ranch - Idaho
Contact
City Clayton
Company Diamond D Ranch Inc.
Contact Thomas & Linda Demorest
City Boise
Company Don's Float Tubing Adventures
Contact Don Lehmen
City Orofino
Company Eakin Ridge Outfitters
Contact Lesley & Lamont Anderson
City Salmon
Company Flying Resort Ranches Inc.
Contact William R. Guth & David E. Williams
City Salmon
Company Gospel Mountain Outfitters
Contact Jim Daude
City Lucile
Company Granite Creek Guest Ranch
Contact Carl & Nessie Zitlau
City Ririe
Company Guth (Norman H) Inc.
Contact Norman H Guth & Mel Reingold
City Salmon
Company Happy Hollow Vacations
Contact Martin & Almira Capps
City Salmon
Company Heinrich & Smith Outfitters
Contact William Heinrich & Robert Smith
City Orofino
Company Hidden Creek Ranch
Contact Iris & John Behr
City Harrison
Company High Desert Enterprises
Contact Andrede & Chris Maisel
City Preston
Company High Desert Expeditions
Contact Rodger Tiffany
City Twins Falls
Company High Llama Wilderness Tours, Inc.
Contact Cutler Umbach
City McCall
Company Horse Creek Outfitters, Inc.
Contact Jim Thomas & Rick Trusnovec
City Challis
Company Huckleberry Heaven Lodge
Contact
City Elk River
Company Idaho Rocky Mountain Ranch
Contact Sandra Beckwith
City Stanley
Company Idaho Whitetail Guides
Contact Jack M. Skille
City Princeton
Company Indian Creek Ranch Inc.
Contact Jack W. Briggs
City North Fork
Company Jarbidge Wilderness Guide & Packing
Contact Lowell & Diane Prunty
City Rogerson
Company Keating Outfitters
Contact Earl R. & Sue Ann Keating, Jr.
City Gibbonsville
Company Lemburg's Priest Lake Outfitters
Contact Randall Lemburg
City Nordman
Company Lochsa River Outfitters
Contact Sherry & Jacey Nygaard
City Potlatch
Company Loon Creek Ranch Inc.
Contact Lyle M. Thomas
City Ellis
Company Lost Lakes Outfitters Inc.
Contact Albert & Diane Latch
City Kooskia
Company Mackay Bar Corporation
Contact Vince Ivanoff
City Boise
Company Middlefork Ranch Inc.
Contact Jimm Sullivan & Bill Widgren
City Boise
Company Mile Hi Outfitters Inc.
Contact Jerry Jeppson & Cliff Zielke
City Challis
Company N ID Border Ranch Oftr. & Guide Serv.
Contact Ardella E. Book
City Sandpoint
Company North Star Outfitters
Contact Kenneth Wolfinbarger & Les Udy
City Challis
Company Ospry Adventures
Contact Cheryl Bransford
City White Bird
Company Quarter Circle A Outfitters
Contact Rick Hussey
City Salmon
Company Redfish Lake Lodge
Contact Jack See
City Stanley
Company Renshaw Outfitting, Inc.
Contact Jim & Lynda Renshaw
City Kamiah
Company Rider Ranch
Contact
City Coeur d'Alene
Company River Mountain Wildlife Experiences
Contact Shannon Lindsey
City White Bird
Company Robson Outfitters
Contact Gary & Marlene Robson
City Felt
Company Rudeen Ranches
Contact Kent A. Rudeen
City American Falls
Company Saddle Springs Trophy Outfitters
Contact Bruce Cole
City Salmon
Company Salmon River Lodge Inc.
Contact Jim Dartt
City Salmon
Company Seven Devils Ranch
Contact Rich & Judy Cook
City Council
Company Sevy Guide Service, Inc.
Contact Robert J. Sevy
City Stanley
Company Shattuck Creek Ranch & Outfitters
Contact Andre Molsee
City Elk River
Company Shepp Ranch
Contact Virginia Hopfenbeck
City Boise
Company Shepp Ranch Idaho
Contact Jinny Hopfenbeck & Paul Resnick
City Boise
Company Sleeping Deer Outfitters Inc.
Contact Ronald J. Clark
City Challis
Company Small Cattle Company
Contact Butch and Sheila Small
City Dubois
Company South Fork Outfitters
Contact Ralph L. Hatter
City Grangeville
Company Stanley Potts Outfitters
Contact Stan & Joy Potts
City Shoup
Company Steel Mountain Outfitters
Contact Ronald L. Sherer
City Eagle
Company Super Outfitting Adventures
Contact James Super
City Bellvue
Company T.J. Outfitting
Contact Tom L. Jarvis
City Challis
Company Taylor Ranch Outfitters
Contact Steve Zettel
City Challis
Company Teton Ridge Ranch
Contact Sandy & Mary Mason
City Tetonia
Company Teton Valley Lodge, Inc.
Contact Randy & Sandy Berry
City Driggs
Company Three Forks' Safaris
Contact Tuck Russell
City Garden Valley
Company Three Rivers Resort & Campground
Contact George Michael Smith
City Kooskia
Company Twin Peaks Ranch Inc.
Contact Eleanor Wisner-Manager
City Salmon
Company Venture Outdoors
Contact Dave Markham & Sue Barney
City Hailey

Company Warm Springs Outfitters
Contact Gordon E. Frost
City Lenore
Company Western Frontier Adventures
Contact Richard A. Hankins
City Mackay
Company Western Pleasure Guest Ranch
Contact
City Sandpoint
Company Whiskey Mountain Outfitters
Contact James I. Bass
City Murphy
Company Whitewater Outfitters
Contact Zeke & Erlene West
City Kamiah
Company Whitewater Wilderness Lodge
Contact
City Cascade
Company Wild Horse Creek Ranch
Contact Dan Mulick - Manager
City Mackay
Company Wilderness Outfitters
Contact Shelda, Justin & Jerrod Farr Scott
City Challis
Company Wilderness Outfitters
Contact Podsaid & Hart
City Coeur d'Alene
Company Willey Ranch Outfitters/ B & B Davis
Contact Buzz Davis
City Boise
Company Wind River Outfitters
Contact Michael and Jaylene Branson
City New Plymouth
Company Yellow Wolf Ranch
Contact Edd S. Woslum
City White Bird

Illinois

Company Northern Illinois Outfitters
Contact Jerry DeVries
City Sandwich

Kansas

Company Diamond V Ranch
Contact Thomas P. Sollner
City Burdick
Company Goose Creek Guide Service
Contact Bruce S. Shultz
City Arlington
Company Hedrick Exotic Animal Farm & B&B Inn
Contact Joe & Sondra Hedrick/Loretta Bailey
City Nickerson
Company JMT Outfitters
Contact Tim Mercer
City Carbondale
Company K R Outfitting
Contact Kim Reyer
City Strong City
Company Milligan Brand Outfitters
Contact Carl A. Morgan
City Altoona
Company Oak Valley Guide Service
Contact William F. Shank
City Independence
Company R L Guide Services
Contact Robert E. Landrum
City Wichita
Company R M F Guide Service
Contact Ronald M. Ford
City Manhattan
Company Servant Guiding
Contact Larry D. Thatcher
City Mulvane
Company Walkers Guide Service
Contact Everett H. Walker
City Wichita

Kentucky

Company Boitnott Guide Service
Contact Billy Joe Boitnott
City Princeton
Company Leech's Guide Service
Contact Jim Leech
City Princeton
Company Sportsman's Quest
Contact Henry Joe Lyon
City Gilbertsville

Louisiana

Company Michikamau Outfitting
Contact
City Churchill Falls
Company Pintail
Contact Lloyd G. Hoover
City Shreveport
Company Tall Timbers Lodge
Contact Judy Davis
City Homer
Company True North Outfitting Co.
Contact Winston White
City Happy Valley - Goose Bay

Maine

Company 9 Lake Outfitters
Contact Edward Richard
City Blaine
Company Allagash Canoe Trips
Contact
City Greenville
Company Ashland Bear Camps
Contact Boyd Ward
City Bucksport
Company Bear Creek Guide Service & Lodge
Contact John Schmidt
City Island Falls
Company Beaver Creek Guide Service
Contact Paul Behring
City Beaver Cove
Company Beech Nut Sporting Camps
Contact Dan & Margaret LaPointe
City Masardis
Company Beech Ridge Guide Service
Contact Glenn Ricker
City Brownville
Company Big Country Guide Service
Contact Russell Cummings
City Augusta
Company Birch Hill Guide Service
Contact Steven Botelho
City Wytopitlock
Company Cedar Ridge Outfitters
Contact Hal and Debbie Blood
City Jackman
Company Conklin's Lodge & Camps
Contact Lester Conklin
City Patten
Company Crooked Tree Lodge & Camps
Contact Nick Curtis
City Portage Lake
Company Crooked-Eye Camp
Contact Kenneth Robinson
City Springfield
Company Dave Tobey Guide & Outfitter
Contact Dave Tobey
City Grand Lake Stream
Company Dean's Den
Contact Dean Paisley
City Eagle Lake
Company Dri-Ki Lodge
Contact Robert & Carrie Keim
City Patten
Company God's Country Guide Service
Contact Leonard Coover
City Brownville
Company Green Mountain Guide & Charter Service
Contact Bill Strout
City Bar Harbor
Company Harry's Lodge
Contact Ed Harris
City Kingman
Company Matagamon Wilderness Campground
Contact Donald Dudley
City Patten
Company Meadow Mountain Guide Service
Contact Robert Sanborn
City Orland
Company Moosehead Adventures
Contact
City Dover-Foxcroft
Company Mount Chase Lodge
Contact Richard Hill
City Patten
Company Mt. Henry Guide Service

Contact Rick Lausier
City Bridgton
Company Nelson Cole & Son
Contact Nelson Cole
City Thorndike
Company North Country Lodge
Contact Dale Goodman
City Patten
Company North Ridge Outfitters
Contact Maynard Pierce Jr.
City Lincolnville
Company Northeast Anglers
Contact Gary D. Scavette
City Northport
Company PB Guide Service
Contact Paul Beauregard
City Skowhegan
Company Raven Retreat
Contact
City Milbridge
Company Remote Maine Tent Hunts
Contact Dan Legere
City Greenville
Company Rivers Bend Camps
Contact Sheldon Lyons
City Masardis
Company Rocky Ridge Guide Service
Contact Carl Bois
City Lovell
Company Snowy River Adventures
Contact Claude Rounds
City Readfield
Company Southern Maine Guide Service
Contact
City Limerick
Company Stony Brook Outfitters
Contact Robert Parker
City Farmington
Company Sundown Cabins
Contact Patrick & Shirley Dubord
City Rockwood
Company The Bradford Camps
Contact
City Ashland
Company The Enchanted Sporting Camps
Contact Don Burnham
City West Forks
Company The Last Resort Hunting & Fishing
Contact Ellen & Tim Casey
City Jackman
Company Track Down Kennel & Lodge
Contact Joel Guimond
City Soldier Pond
Company Turnpike Ridge Outfitters
Contact Don Helstrom Jr.
City Medway
Company Umc'olc'us
Contact Al & Audrey Currier
City Oxbow
Company Western Mountain Hunter's Service
Contact Ronald Rackliff
City Temple
Company Wilderness Sports
Contact Clark Wormell
City Carmel
Company Wilds of Maine Guide Service
Contact Michael Patterson
City Yarmouth
Company Wilsons
Contact Shan & Wayne Snell
City Greenville
Company Woody's
Contact Woody & Elsie Martin
City Rockwood

Maryland

Company F & M Ranch Outfitting
Contact Floyd W. Price
City Kennedyville
Company Mark Kovach Fishing Services
Contact Mark E. Kovach
City Silver Spring

Massachusetts

Company Duke's Butternut Cabin & Guide Service
Contact Lee Duke
City Fall River
Company High Island Ranch
Contact George Nelson Jr.
City Georgetown
Company Rol-Yat Guide Service
Contact George Taylor
City Ludlow

Michigan

Company Trail Creek Lodge
Contact Ralph Mersdorf
City Bay City
Company Wildcat Creek Outfitters
Contact Russell L. Newton III
City Grand Rapids

Minnesota

Company Liard River Outfitters
Contact Bob Johnson
City Buffalo
Company Misaw Lake Lodge
Contact Bob & Shar Johnson
City Brooklyn Park
Company Moose Creek Outfitters
Contact Rodney Paulson
City Shevlin
Company Udovich Guide Service
Contact Dennis Udovich
City Gheen

Mississippi

Company Brushy Creek Guest Ranch
Contact
City Gloster
Company Deep South Wilderness Outfitters
Contact James Goss
City Hollandale
Company Delta National Guide Service
Contact Jim Wilson
City Greenville
Company Wildlife Inc.
Contact
City Schlater

Missouri

Company Farley's International Adventures
Contact William G. Farley
City Kirksville
Company Fraley Ranch
Contact Tom Fraley
City Newburg
Company Herefordale Ranch
Contact Curtis Sidwell
City Queen City
Company Walker Outfitters
Contact Larry Walker
City Nevada

Montana

Company "Beyond All Roads" Klicks K Bar L
Contact
City Augusta
Company 320 Ranch
Contact Pat Sage-Mgr.
City Gallatin Gateway
Company 7 Lazy P Ranch
Contact Chuck Blixrud
City Choteau
Company 7-V Ranch
Contact Ross & Kelly Childers
City Brusett
Company 7W Guest Ranch
Contact Glenda S. Reynolds
City Sand Springs
Company A Lazy H Outfitters
Contact Allen & Sally Haas
City Choteau
Company Absaroka Outfitters
Contact Vernon T. Smith
City Emigrant
Company American Hunting Services

Contact Guy Shanks
City Bigfork
Company Anchor Outfitting
Contact Charles M. Rein
City Big Timber
Company Antlers Guide Service
Contact George H. Athas
City Gardiner
Company Anvil Butte Ranch
Contact
City Billings
Company Atcheson Outfitting
Contact John D. "Jack" Atcheson
City Butte
Company Avalanche Basin Outfitters
Contact Douglas Caltrider
City White Sulphur Springs
Company Averill's Flathead Lake Lodge
Contact Doug & Maureen Averill
City Bigfork
Company Badland Buck & Bull Outfitters
Contact Lee A. Zeller
City Miles City
Company Bar N Ranch
Contact
City West Yellowstone
Company Bar Y Seven Ranch
Contact Claude Saylor
City Brusett
Company Barlett Creek Outfitters
Contact Mike Smith
City Deer Lodge
Company Battle Creek Lodge
Contact
City Choteau
Company Bear Creek Outfitters & Guest Ranch
Contact Bill Beck
City Cut Bank
Company Bear Creek Ranch
Contact Bill Beck
City Cutbank
Company Bear Paw Outfitters
Contact Tim Bowers
City Livingston
Company Bear Trap Outfitters
Contact Kenneth R. Whitman
City West Yellowstone
Company Beartooth Plateau Outfitters, Inc.
Contact Ronnie L. Wright
City Cooke City
Company Benchmark Wilderness Guest Ranch
Contact Darwin C. Heckman
City Augusta
Company Big "M" Outfitters
Contact Robert E. Hogue
City Philipsburg
Company Big Cir Outfitters & Lodge
Contact Stanley A. Cirspinski
City DeBorgia
Company Big Sky Expeditions
Contact Joel S. Wiemer
City Missoula
Company Big Sky Outfitters
Contact Richard F Kountz
City Bozeman
Company Big Sky Roping Ranch
Contact
City Huntley
Company Big Sky Trophy Outfitters
Contact Sam C. Borla
City Forsyth
Company Big Timber Guides
Contact Robert J. Bovee
City Big Timber
Company Bighorn Country Outfitters
Contact George Kelly
City Ft. Smith
Company Billingsley Ranch Outfitters
Contact Jack Billingsley
City Glasgow
Company Black Otter Guide Service
Contact Duane Neal
City Pray
Company Blizzard Mountain Outfitters
Contact Nicholas Smetana
City Wolf Creek
Company Blue Nugget Outfitters
Contact Eugene R. Knight
City Utica
Company Blue Ribbon Flies
Contact Craig R. Mathews
City West Yellowstone
Company Blue Ridge Outfitters
Contact Earl Ray Shores
City Malta
Company Blue Rock Outfitters
Contact O. Kurt Hughes
City Miles City
Company Blue Spruce Lodge & Guest Ranch
Contact
City Trout Creek
Company Bonanza Creek Country
Contact
City Martinsdale
Company Borderline Outfitters
Contact Miles Hutton
City Turner
Company Boulder River Ranch
Contact
City McLeod
Company Broken Arrow Lodge
Contact Erwin & Sherry Clark
City Alder
Company Broken V Guest Ranch
Contact
City Roundup
Company Buck Creek Ranch Guide Service
Contact Thomas W. Parker
City Condon
Company Buckhorn Ranch Outfitters
Contact Harry T. Workman
City Eureka
Company Buffalo Creek Ranch
Contact
City Custer
Company Buffalo Jump Outfitting, LLC
Contact
City Cameron
Company Bull Lake Guest Ranch
Contact
City Troy
Company Bull Mountain Outfitters
Contact M.J. "Mike" Murphy
City Joliet
Company Bull Run Outfitters & Guest Ranch
Contact Joe Tripp
City Cascade
Company Bullseye Outfitting
Contact Jeff Smith
City Trout Creek
Company Burke Ranch
Contact Don J. Burke
City Glasgow
Company Burns Creek Outfitters
Contact Alan R. Klempel
City Bloomfield
Company Butler Outfitters
Contact H. Earl Butler
City Darby
Company C-Bar Heart Guest Ranch & Lodge
Contact
City Coram
Company Cabin Creek Outfitters
Contact Kenneth W. Phillips
City Ravalli
Company Cabinet Divide Outfitters
Contact Terry N. Kayser
City Noxon
Company Cabinet Mountain Outfitters
Contact Gerald & Vikki Carr
City Plains
Company Camp Creek Inn B & B Guest Ranch
Contact
City Sula
Company Canyon & Creek Outfitters
Contact Lyle S. Bainbridge
City Stevensville
Company Canyon Creek Guest Ranch
Contact David L. Duncan
City Melrose
Company Canyon Creek Ranch
Contact
City Melrose
Company Careless Creek Getaway
Contact
City Shawmut
Company Carl Mann's Montana Experience Outfitter
Contact Carl A. Mann
City Lolo
Company Castle Lodge
Contact D. Castle Smith
City Emigrant
Company Cayuse Outfitters
Contact Larry A. Lahren
City Livingston
Company CB Cattle & Guest Ranch
Contact
City Cameron
Company Centennial Guest Ranch
Contact Tim Beardsley
City Ennis
Company Centennial Outfitters
Contact Mel W. Montgomery
City Lima
Company Central Montana Outfitters

Contact Chad S. Schearer
City Great Falls
Company Chase Hill Outfitters
Contact Bill & Renita Brown
City Big Sandy
Company Cheff Guest Ranch
Contact Mick & Karen Cheff
City Charlo
Company Chris Branger, Outfitter
Contact Chris W. Branger
City Roscoe
Company Circle KBL Outfitters
Contact Scott Boulanger
City Victor
Company Clearwater Outfitters
Contact Tom Ziberman
City Stevensville
Company Clearwater Outfitters
Contact Larry J. Kenney
City Seeley Lake
Company Cougar Ranch Outfitters
Contact Buck Wood
City Big Arm
Company Cougar Ridge Outdoors
Contact William Richard Briggs
City Dell
Company Covered Wagon Ranch
Contact
City Gallatin Gateway
Company Coyote Outfitters
Contact Donald E. Mawyer
City Twin Bridges
Company Crow Creek Outfitters & Guides
Contact Michael E. Parsons
City Toston
Company Daystar Guest Ranch
Contact
City West Glacier
Company DC Outfitting
Contact Richard L. Cox
City Lewistown
Company Dead Rock Guest Ranch
Contact
City Clyde Park
Company Donohoe Outfitting
Contact Paul T. Donohoe
City Nye
Company Double Shot Doc Ranch
Contact
City Columbus
Company Double Spear Ranch
Contact Tony and Donna Blackmore
City Pryor
Company DRGA Ranch
Contact
City Ismay
Company East Boulder River Guest House
Contact
City Big Timber
Company East Fork Outfitters
Contact Mark McKee
City Victor
Company Ed Curnow Outfitters
Contact Edward E. Curnow
City Cameron
Company Elk Creek Outfitting
Contact Brent & Kathy Fitchett
City Heron
Company Elk Horn Enterprises
Contact Pete Clark
City Big Timber
Company Elk Ridge Outfitters
Contact Doug & Michelle Landers
City Wilsall
Company Elkhorn Outfitters
Contact Henry T. Barron
City Townsend
Company Elkhorn Ranch
Contact Linda Miller
City Gallatin Gateway
Company Esper's Under Wild Skies Lodge & Outfitters
Contact Vaughn and Judy Esper
City Phillipsburg
Company EW Watson & Sons Outfitting
Contact Ed and Wanda Watson
City Townsend
Company Flying Diamond Guide Service
Contact Jack W.P. Davis
City Livingston
Company Flying Eagle Ranch
Contact Wayne H. Mackie
City Coram
Company Flying W Outfitters
Contact Sherry Ann Ward
City Custer
Company Ford Creek Outfitters
Contact Elizabeth Barker
City Augusta
Company Four Six Outfitters
Contact Fred Ennist
City Pony
Company Gary Webb Guide & Outfitters
Contact Gary Webb
City Darby
Company George Klemens Outfitting
Contact George C. Klemens
City White Sulphur Springs
Company God's Country Ourtitters
Contact Shane & Bridgitt Erickson
City Lincoln
Company Golden Bear Outfitters
Contact Walter C. & Una Earl
City Judith Gap
Company Great Basin Hunters
Contact Gerald Nyman
City Helena
Company Great Bear Outfitters
Contact H.J. Gilchrist
City Great Falls
Company Great Divide Guiding/ Outfitters
Contact Richard T. Jackson
City East Glacier
Company Greyson Creek Meadows Rec.
Contact Ted Flynn
City Townsend
Company Gunsel Horse Adventures-MT Divison
Contact Scott Hayes
City Augusta
Company Hailstone Ranch Co.
Contact Samuel Langhus
City Big Timber
Company Hargrave Cattle & Guest Ranch
Contact Leo and Ellen Hargrave
City Marion
Company Hawkins Outfitters
Contact Steve Hawkins
City Eureka
Company Heaven on Earth Ranch
Contact
City Great Falls
Company Hidden Hollow Hidaway Ranch
Contact Gary Flynn
City Townsend
Company Hidden Hollow Hideaway
Contact Kelly & Jill Flynn
City Townsend
Company Hildreth Livestock Ranch
Contact
City Dillon
Company Hill's Professional Outfitters
Contact Edna V. Hill
City Trout Creek
Company Homestead Ranch
Contact Ed & Billie Lou Arnott
City Hobson
Company Horse Prairie Guest Ranch
Contact Mack & Candi Hedges
City Dillon
Company Horse Prairie Outfitters
Contact Tom Pierce
City Dillon
Company I.C.R. Outfitters
Contact Wade Warren Durham
City Cameron
Company Iron Horse Outfitters
Contact Art Griffith
City Hamilton
Company Iron Wheel Ranch
Contact John and Sherry Cargill
City Whitehall
Company J & J Guide Service
Contact Jamie & Juanita Byrne
City Mill Iron
Company Jackson-Snyder Ranch
Contact
City Lewistown
Company JJJ Wilderness Ranch
Contact Max & Ann Barker
City Augusta
Company JM Bar Outfitters
Contact Jeffery & Maria Freeman
City Clinton
Company Joe Heimer Outfitting
Contact Joseph A. Heimer
City Livingston
Company Johnson Outfitters
Contact Kathryn M. Johnson
City Gardiner
Company Josephson Outfitting
Contact Edward & Elisa Josephson
City Plains
Company JR/Buffalo Creek Outfitters
Contact John W. Robidou
City Gardiner
Company Jumping Rainbow Ranch
Contact
City Livingston

Company Keenan Ranch/Bugle Ridge Outfitters
Contact
City Emigrant
Company Kent "Jake" Grimm
Contact Kent D. Grimm
City Gallatin Gateway
Company Kootenai High Country Hunting
Contact David Hayward
City Eureka
Company L Diamond E Ranch
Contact Dan J. Ekstrom
City Clinton
Company Lake Upsata Guest Ranch
Contact
City Ovando
Company Lapham Outfitters
Contact Max & Debbie Lapham
City Jackson
Company Laughing Water Ranch
Contact Ted & Holly Mikita-Finch
City Fortine
Company Lazy E-L Working Guest Ranch
Contact
City Roscoe
Company Lazy Heart Outfitters
Contact Linda M. Budeski
City Livingston
Company Lazy K Bar Ranch
Contact
City Big Timber
Company Lazy T4 Outfitters
Contact Spencer G. Trogdon
City Victor
Company Lion Creek Outfitters
Contact Cecil L Noble
City Kalispell
Company Lochsa Lodge Resort
Contact
City Lolo
Company Lone Tree Outfitting & Guide Service
Contact Larry A. Pendleton
City Stevensville
Company Lonesome Spur Guest Ranch
Contact
City Bridger
Company Lost Creek Outfitters
Contact Don O. Wright
City Livingston
Company Lost Creek Outfitting
Contact James Leslie Haynie
City Circle
Company Lost Spur Working Ranch
Contact
City Willard
Company M Hanging Cross Outfitters & Guide
Contact Michael "Chip" Gollehon
City Bynum
Company Mandorla Ranch
Contact
City St. Ignatius
Company McClain Guest House
Contact
City Bozeman
Company McFarland & White Ranch
Contact Gilbert White
City Two Dot
Company Medicine Lake Outfitters
Contact Thomas M. Heintz
City Bozeman
Company Milller Outfitters
Contact Robert E. Miller
City Great Falls
Company Mills Outfitting
Contact Tucker Miller
City Augusta
Company Ming Coulee Outfitters
Contact James M. Gasvoda
City Sand Coulee
Company Missouri Breaks Adventures
Contact John E. Vaia
City Lewistown
Company Mitchell Outfitting
Contact Floyd W. Mitchell
City Broadus
Company Montana High Country Outfitter
Contact Timothy R. Reishus
City Noxon
Company Montana Outfitter
Contact Alfred S. Bassett
City Melstone
Company Montana Trail Trophy Outfitter
Contact Michael J. Clark
City Clyde Park
Company Monture Face Outfitters
Contact Tom Ide and Valerie Call
City Greenough
Company Morgan Guest House
Contact
City Bozeman
Company Mossy Horn Outfitters
Contact Gordon W. Sampson
City Whitehall
Company Mountain Sky Guest Ranch
Contact Shirley Arnesault
City Bozeman
Company Mountain Trail Outfitters
Contact David B. Gamble
City Livingston
Company Muleshoe Outfitters & Guide Service
Contact Jack Howser
City Deer Lodge
Company Neal Outfitter's
Contact Danielle Neal
City Augusta
Company Nez Perce Ranch
Contact
City Darby
Company Nine Quarter Circle Guest Ranch
Contact Kim and Kelly Kelsey
City Gallatin Gateway
Company North Star Outfitters
Contact Everett "EB" Morris
City Forsyth
Company North Yellowstone Outfitters
Contact William H. Hoppe
City Gardner
Company Painted Rock Outfitters
Contact Mike & Debbie Rodgers
City Darby
Company Parade Rest Guest Ranch
Contact
City West Yellowstone
Company Paradise Outfitters
Contact Jim H. Cooper
City Billings
Company Parson's Outfitting
Contact Jean Parsons
City Cascade
Company Paul Roos Outfitters
Contact Paul S. Roos
City Helena
Company Paul Tunkis Flyfishing Guide Service
Contact Paul Tunkis
City Livingston
Company Pelly Lake Wilderness Outfitters
Contact Dennis LeVeque
City Cascade
Company Pepperbox Ranch
Contact
City Darby
Company Pig Eye Outfitters
Contact Peter B. Rogers
City Utica
Company Pine Butte Guest Ranch
Contact
City Choteau
Company Pine Hills Outfitters
Contact Mike Barthelmess
City Swan Valley
Company Pioneer Outfitter
Contact Cliff & Carolyn Page
City Wise River
Company Point of Rocks Guest Ranch
Contact Irvin "Max" Chase
City Emigrant
Company R.L. Sourbrine Outfit. & Sons
Contact Richard L. Sourbrine
City Victor
Company Ram Mountain Outfitters
Contact Robert L Neal
City Philipsburg
Company Ramshorn Outfitters
Contact Audie & Vivianne Anderson
City Townsend
Company Range Riders Ranch
Contact Terry & Wyoma Terland
City Reed Point
Company Rawhide Guide Service
Contact Leroy A. Fatouros
City Livingston
Company Rawhide Guide Service
Contact Don Degroft
City White Sulpher Springs
Company Ray Perkins Outfitter
Contact J. Ray Perkins
City Miles City
Company Redbone Outfitting
Contact Carl "Bud" Martin
City Florence
Company Reynolds Hollowtop Hideaway
Contact Harvey D. Reynolds
City Dillon
Company Rich Ranch
Contact Jack & Belinda Rich

City Seeley Lake
Company Rick Wemple Outfitting/ Wildlife Adv.
Contact Richard J. Wemple
City Victor
Company Rimrock Ridge Outfitters
Contact Roy L. Coneen
City White Sulphur Springs
Company River Breaks Outfitting
Contact Rick R. Wood
City Lewistown
Company River Quest Angler
Contact Bob Swain
City Columbus
Company RJR Ranch
Contact
City Eureka
Company Robert Butler Outfitting
Contact Robert G. Butler
City Twin Bridges
Company Rock'n 7C Outfitters
Contact Dennis & Jane Chatlain
City Red Lodge
Company Rocky Mountain Adventures
Contact Daniel J. Shoemaker
City Hamilton
Company Rose Ranch
Contact
City Ekalaka
Company Rugg's Outfitting
Contact Raymond Rugg
City Superior
Company Rumph Ranch Outfitters
Contact Richard N. Rumph
City Biddle
Company Running Waters Ranch
Contact Bruce E. Funk
City Bigfork
Company Rus Willis Outfitting
Contact Richard K. Willis
City Noxon
Company Rush's Lake View Ranch
Contact Kevin Rush
City Marshall
Company S & W Outfitters
Contact Brad D. Hanzel
City Big Sky
Company Sage & Sun Outfitting
Contact David J. Patts
City Forsyth
Company Scapegoat Wilderness Outfitter
Contact William M. Plante
City Fort Benton
Company Selway Bitterroot Outfitters
Contact Dave Hettinger
City Hamilton
Company Seven Bar Cross Ranch
Contact Dale W. Williams
City Sonnette
Company Shadow Basin Outfitters
Contact
City Hamilton
Company Shields Valley Outfitters
Contact Gregory L. Cissel
City Livingston
Company Shining Mountain Outfitters
Contact Paul K. Johnson
City Billings
Company Shining Times Outfitting
Contact Richard Steve Vetsch
City Townsend
Company Shores Outfitting
Contact Eric R. Shores
City Cameron
Company Silver Bow Outfitters
Contact Leonard Howells
City Libby
Company Silver Creek Outfitters
Contact Chad Hoover
City Big Timber
Company Silverwolf Chalet Resort
Contact James & Bonnie Kennedy
City Bozeman
Company Skyline Guest Ranch & Guide
Contact Victor Jackson
City Cooke City
Company Skyline Outfitters & Wilderness Lodge
Contact Cameron E. Lee
City Hungry Horse
Company Skyview Ranch
Contact
City Big Sandy
Company Snowline Outfitters
Contact Patrick G. Sinclair
City Jordan
Company Spotted Bear Ranch
Contact H. William Armstrong
City West Glacier
Company Story Cattle Co. & Outfitting
Contact Michael Story
City Emigrant
Company Sugarloaf Mountain Outfitters
Contact William Ray Flanagan
City Absarokee
Company Sunburst Adventures
Contact Terry C. Johnson
City Bozeman
Company Sundance Ranch
Contact
City Ovando
Company Sunset Guest Ranch
Contact Mike C. McCormick
City Helmville
Company Sweet Grass Ranch
Contact
City Big Timber
Company Tate's Upper Canyon Ranch
Contact Donna & Jake McDonald
City Alder
Company The Elkhorn Guest Ranch
Contact
City Clinton
Company The Seventh Ranch
Contact
City Garryowen
Company The Stoney Lonesome Ranch
Contact
City Absarokee
Company The Tom Miner Lodge
Contact John A. Keenan
City Emigrant
Company The Wald Ranch
Contact
City Lodge Grass
Company Three Cross Ranch
Contact Dan and Arleene Weppler
City Ryegate
Company Thunder Bow Outfitters
Contact Ron Robinson
City Condon
Company Toussaint Ranch
Contact
City Wise River
Company Track Outfitters & Guide Service
Contact Johnny C. McGee
City Livingston
Company TriMountain Outfitters
Contact Andy Celander
City White Sulphur Springs
Company Triple Creek Ranch
Contact
City Darby
Company Triple Tree Ranch
Contact William L. Myers
City Boulder
Company Upper Canyon Outfitters
Contact Donna Tate MacDonald
City Alder
Company Vanhaur Polled Hereford Ranch
Contact
City Hilger
Company Vikings Mountain Ranch
Contact Douglas K. Knutson
City Kalispell
Company Wayne Hill Outfitting
Contact Wayne Hill
City Noxon
Company West Fork Meadows Ranch, Inc.
Contact
City Darby
Company Whiskey Ridge Outfitter's
Contact Steven R. Knox
City Winifred
Company White Buffalo Ranch Retreat
Contact
City Yellowtail
Company Why Lazy Tee Ranch
Contact
City Stockett
Company Wickens Salt Creek Ranch
Contact
City Hilger
Company Wild West Outfitters
Contact Michael A. Goyins
City Helena
Company Williams Outfitters
Contact Harry L. Williams
City Kalispell
Company Willow Ranch
Contact Storrs M. Bishop
City Ennis
Company Willow Springs Outfitters
Contact Gordon L. Patton
City Cameron
Company Wolf Mountain Ranch
Contact
City Billings
Company Wolfpack Outfitters
Contact Jeffrey Wingard

City Ennis
Company World Class Outfitting Adventures
Contact Jason D. & Carolyn Clinkenbeard
City Arlee
Company WTR Outfitters
Contact Karen Hooker
City Ovando
Company X-A Ranch
Contact Boland Clark
City McLeod
Company Yellowstone Mountain Guides
Contact Steven R. Gamble
City Bozeman
Company Yellowstone Valley Ranch
Contact
City Livingston
Company ZAK Inn Guest Ranch
Contact
City Sheridan
Company ZW Ranch
Contact Calvin & Lorrie Zimdars
City Polaris

Nebraska

Company Chesley's Lodge
Contact Dave & Jo Chesley & Sons
City Callaway
Company Flying A Ranch
Contact Marlene Striegal
City Trenton
Company Heartland Outfitters
Contact Kelly & Rose Hildebrandt
City Valentine
Company Merritt Trading Post Resort
Contact Jon & Marian Davenport
City Valentine
Company Sandhills Adventures
Contact Delten Rhoades
City Brewster
Company The Pines
Contact John Kurtz
City Long Pine
Company The Twisted Pine Ranch
Contact Ken & Sharon Moreland
City Merriman
Company Trapper's Creek Outdoors
Contact Gary & Mary Hughes
City Burwell

Nevada

Company Black Rock Outfitters
Contact Michael J. Hornbarger
City Winnemucca
Company Blackrock Outfitters
Contact Henry K. Arrien II
City Winnemucca
Company D/G Outfitters
Contact Eric Dalen
City Reno
Company Elko Guide Service
Contact William S. Gibson
City Elko
Company George Flournoy Outfitting
Contact George Flournoy
City Sun Valley
Company High Desert Outfitters
Contact Steven J. DeRicco
City Las Vegas
Company Hunewill Guest Ranch
Contact
City Wellington
Company Monument Canyon Ranch
Contact
City Sparks
Company Nevada Desert Trophy Hunts
Contact Roy Lerg
City Smith
Company Nevada High Country Outfitters
Contact Paul D. Bottari
City Wells
Company Nevada High Desert Outfitters
Contact William B. Watega
City Reno
Company Pine Forest Hunt Club & Guide Service
Contact Laurence Montero
City Winnemucca
Company Secret Pass Outfitters
Contact Stephen G. Wright
City Ruby Valley
Company Silver State Guides & Outfitters
Contact Elvin W. Cronister
City Las Vegas
Company Silver State Guides & Outfitters
Contact Phillip E. Trousdale
City Pioche
Company Southern Nevada/Utah Outfitter
Contact Boyd J. Wittwer
City Bunkerville
Company Southern Nevada/Utah Outfitter
Contact Harold Wittwer
City Mesquite
Company The Great Ripoff Guide Service
Contact James A. & Robert R. Combs
City N. Las Vegas
Company Virgil's Desert Bighorn Hunts
Contact John V. Zenz
City Sparks
Company White River Guide Service
Contact Mark A. Lane
City Ely

New Hampshire

Company Untamed Wilderness
Contact Mark Stilkey
City Epping

New Mexico

Company 5 M Outfitters
Contact Bruce Maker
City Chama
Company Adventures in the Great Outdoors
Contact Tom Schubring
City Ranchos de Taos
Company Al Johnson Outfitters
Contact Al Johnson
City Taos Ski Valley
Company All American Outfitter/Guide Service
Contact Gaudelli Brandon
City Reserve
Company Baca Outfitters, Inc.
Contact David Collis
City Jemez
Company Back Country Outfitters of New Mexico
Contact Sydney Cates
City Silver City
Company Baldy Mountain Outfitters
Contact H. Gary Blacksten
City Springer
Company Bar X Bar Ranch
Contact
City Pecos
Company Bear Creek Outfitters
Contact Louis Probo
City Silver City
Company Beaverhead Outfitters
Contact Ken C. Swaim
City Magdalena
Company Big Canyon Outfitters
Contact J. David Smoker
City Cimarron
Company Blackfire Flyfishing Guest Ranch
Contact Mickey & Maggie Greenwood
City Angel Fire
Company Bobcat Pass Wilderness Adventures
Contact Henry Lewis
City Red River
Company Boyd's High Timber Hunting
Contact Richard (Buzz) Boyd
City Chama
Company Bull Creek Outfitters
Contact John R. Lucero
City Santa Fe
Company Bulls of Baldy Mountain Guide Service
Contact Art MacKInstry
City Red River
Company Bullseye Outfitter & Guide
Contact Joseph Graham
City Ruidoso
Company Burnt Canyon Outfitter & Guiding Service
Contact John Allen
City Tularosa
Company Butler - Moreno Ranch West
Contact Bobby & Ginni Butler

City Eagle Nest
Company Canadian River Cattle Co.
Contact Joe Roy Ray
City Roy
Company Cecil Ralston Guide & Outfitters
Contact Cecil & Jodie Ralston
City Bernalillo
Company Circle Bar West Ranch
Contact Tony G. Dickinson
City Tinnie
Company Circle S Stables
Contact Kirk Storey
City Glorjeta
Company Cougar Mountain Guide Service
Contact Doug Dobbs
City Corona
Company Cougar Mountain Outfitters
Contact Robert J. Seeds
City Espanola
Company CS Ranch Hunting & Outfitting
Contact Randy Davis
City Cimarron
Company Dark Canyon Outfitters
Contact Howard (Butch) Harris, Jr.
City Alamogordo
Company Dark Timber
Contact Randy Pettingill
City Chama
Company Dirk Neal's Outfitting Service
Contact Dirk Neal
City Red River
Company Double A Outfitters
Contact Andrew Sanchez
City Espanola
Company Down Home
Contact Walter Hobbs
City Virden
Company E.J. Sceery Co.
Contact Ed Sceery
City Santa Fe
Company East Moreno Ranch
Contact Albert Murray & Ron Simmons
City Eagle Nest
Company Garrison Guide & Outfitting
Contact Gary Garrison
City Deming
Company Geronimo's Outfitters
Contact David M. Jiron
City Tatum
Company Gila Wilderness Outfitters
Contact Junior Lewis
City Cliff
Company Gonzales Outfitting Guiding
Contact Thomas Gilbert Gonzales
City San Mateo
Company Guide & Outfitting Service
Contact Ken Cason
City Magdelena
Company H & A Outfitters
Contact Andrew Salgado
City Santa Fe
Company H-J Outfitters
Contact Elvin Post
City Lindrith
Company Halfmoon Outfitters
Contact Dr. Mike Jones
City El Prado
Company Hamwood Guide & Outfitters
Contact Marty Greenwood
City San Antonio
Company Handrich Guide & Outfitters
Contact Dave Handrich
City Glenwood
Company Hartley Guest Ranch
Contact Ray and Doris Hartley
City Roy
Company Henderson Outfitters
Contact Wesley Henderson
City Winston
Company High Country Connections
Contact Casey Veach
City Farmington
Company High Country Outfitters
Contact Anthony B. Montoya
City Cuba
Company High Country Outfitters
Contact Vance Lewis
City Red River
Company High Country Store
Contact Larry M. Sellers
City Jemez Springs
Company Higher Ground Outfitters
Contact Doc Rolston
City Rogers
Company Horizon Guide & Outfitters
Contact Kelly Dow
City Socorro
Company JC Outfitters
Contact Frank Casaus
City Mora
Company Jenco Outfitters
Contact Philip Zwiefelhofer
City Grants
Company Jim Bobb Guide & Outfitter
Contact James Bobb
City Capitan
Company Ken Armenta Guide & Outfitting
Contact Ken Armenta
City Capitan
Company Kennedy Hunting Services
Contact Kirk Kennedy
City Des Moines
Company Kiowa Hunting Service
Contact Tim Barraclough Jr. & Al Cata
City Raton
Company Kit Carson Outfitters
Contact Darrell Bays
City Bloomfield
Company L.J. Armstrong Big Game Outfitter
Contact L.J. Armstrong
City Cliff
Company Lazy BW Outfitters
Contact Bob Ward
City Santa Fe
Company Limestone Outfitters
Contact Chip Welty
City Williamsburg
Company Limestone Outfitters
Contact Darell Welty
City Winston
Company Little Rio Grande Outfitters
Contact Edward T. Duran
City Ranchos de Taos
Company Lyons Ranch
Contact Patrick Lyons
City Cuervo
Company M & M Outfitting
Contact Michael Montoya
City Albuquerque
Company Mangas Outfitters
Contact Tim Geng
City Datil
Company Mark Upshaw Guide Service
Contact Mark Upshaw
City Datal
Company Mark V. Guide Services
Contact Mike Archuleta
City Espanola
Company Martinez Outfitters & Guide Service
Contact Donald Martinez
City Cebolla
Company Maynard Ranch
Contact Perry & Brenda Hunsaker and Billy & Nora Maynard
City Higley, Arizona
Company Michael Root's Guide Service
Contact Michael Root
City Cuchillo
Company Milligan Brand Outfitting
Contact Marvin N. Henry Jr.
City Chama
Company Montana Del Oso Ranch, Inc.
Contact Tim Edwards
City Silver City
Company Moreno Valley Outfitters
Contact Robert Reese
City Eagle Nest
Company Mountain States Guide Service
Contact Rob Degner
City La Plata
Company Mountain View Cabins/Eagle Nest Marina
Contact Jo Finley
City Eagle Nest
Company P Diamond J Outfitters
Contact R.J. Nolen
City McAlister
Company Percha Creek Outfitters
Contact W.A. Williams
City Faircres
Company Pound Bros. Guides & Outfitters
Contact Billy Jack Pound
City Socorro
Company Puerto Ranch Outfitting
Contact Aparcio Herrera
City Cuba
Company Rawhide Outfitters
Contact Rodney Prince
City Raton
Company RB Outfitters & Guide Service
Contact Ronald Schalla
City Bosque
Company Rio Brazos Outfitters
Contact Frank Y. Simms
City Chama
Company Rio Costilla Park
Contact
City Costilla

Company Rio Nutrias Cattle & Hunting
Contact Juan Montano
City Tierra Amarilla
Company Robert I. Hooten
Contact Robert I. Hooten
City Carrizozo
Company Runnels Outfitter Guide Service
Contact Robert Runnels
City Capitan
Company Sagebrush Outfitters
Contact Robert Guerin, Jr.
City Tierra Amarilla
Company San Francisco River Outfitters
Contact Tom Klunker
City Glenwood
Company Sangre de Cristo Outfitters, Inc.
Contact Tony Herrera
City Arroyo Seco
Company Santa Fe Guiding Company
Contact Robert B. King
City Santa Fe
Company Sibley Ranch
Contact Christine Freeman
City Carlsbad
Company Simpson Outfitters
Contact Tom Simpson
City Tularosa
Company Sky Ryders
Contact Kurt J. Lee
City Angel Fire
Company Sofia Outfitters
Contact Roger Manning
City Grenville
Company South Fork Outfitters, Inc.
Contact Michael Grace
City Cleveland
Company Spill Ranch Hunting
Contact Edward R. Spill
City Tierra Amarilla
Company SW New Mexico Outfitters
Contact Nettie Armstrong
City Quemado
Company SW Outfitters & Guide Service, Ltd.
Contact Robert A. Davis, Jr.
City Albuquerque
Company Talisman Hunting
Contact Lonnie Hennigh & Charles Berg
City Tierra Amarilla
Company Tall Tales Guide Services
Contact Sara Jane Evans
City Maxwell
Company Terrero General Store and Riding Stable Inc.
Contact Huie Ley
City Terrero
Company The Pueblo of Laguna
Contact
City Laguna
Company Tierra Blanca Ranch Outfitters
Contact Scott Chandler
City Hillsboro
Company Tierra Encantada Guide/ Outfitter
Contact Roger Gabaldon
City San Antonio
Company Tinnin Enterprises
Contact
City Albuquerque
Company Tomahawk Outfitters
Contact James E. Kneip
City Springer
Company Trail Riders
Contact Susan Johnson
City Magdelena
Company Tri-Me Outfitter
Contact Ronald Ulibarri
City Alcalde
Company Vermejo Park Ranch
Contact Jim Baker
City Raton
Company Way West Outfitters
Contact Keith Reiley
City Datil
Company Zuni Mtn. Guide & Outfitting
Contact Robert Fifer
City Thoreau

New York

Company Algoma East Cottages & Outfitters
Contact Tom Lembke & Family
City West Seneca
Company Blue Mountain Lake Guide Service
Contact Joe Cummins
City Blue Mountain Lake
Company C.P.'s Guiding Service
Contact Chirs Palumbo
City Putnam
Company Catskill Outdoor Adventures
Contact Charles "Sonny" Somelofski
City Andes
Company Cold River Ranch
Contact John Fontana
City Tupper Lake
Company DC Outdoor Adventures
Contact Dennis Caracciolo
City Brentwood
Company Don Brown Guide Service
Contact Don Brown
City Jefferson
Company East Wind
Contact Luke H. Evans
City Oneida
Company Empire Outfitters & Guide Service
Contact James M. Baker
City Pleasant Valley
Company Hemlock Cliff Bed & Breakfast Lodge
Contact William M. Nolis Jr.
City Nichols
Company Hills-A-Vaille
Contact Charles Baldwin
City Westerlo
Company Indian Mountain Lodge
Contact
City Millerton
Company J & J Outdoors
Contact Judd V. Groff
City Wynantskill
Company Kidney Creek Farms & Preserve
Contact Gary Breski
City Schaticoke
Company Limbhanger Lodge
Contact Paul Paduano
City Niagara Falls
Company Mad Dragon Dynasty
Contact Guide Shihan & Pete Traina
City Ridgewood
Company Meadow Brook Guiding
Contact Delbert Ryan
City Harrisville
Company Newell's Guide Service
Contact Gary K. Newell
City Gainesville
Company North Country Outfitters
Contact Barney & Bob & Rick Mundy
City Levittown
Company Pepperbox Outfitters
Contact Jack Finklea
City Beaver River
Company Pinegrove Dude Ranch
Contact David O'Halloran
City Kerhonkson
Company Placid Bay Ventures Guide & Charter Svc.
Contact Capt. Uwe Herb Dramm
City Lake Placid
Company Plateau Guide Service
Contact Wayne Kwasniewski
City West Leyden
Company R. L. C. Services
Contact Roland (Rollie) Card
City Chenango Forks
Company Sam Orne Adventures
Contact Sam Orne
City Valatie
Company Stillwaters Guide Service
Contact Terry Watson
City Lake Placid
Company Temagami Riverside Lodge
Contact Roger Watson & Tom Dorr
City Clarence Center
Company Tightlines Guide Service
Contact Donald Kingsley
City Pulaski
Company Trailhead Lodge
Contact John & Michael Washburn
City Northville
Company Walleye Wizard Guide Service
Contact Bill Struble
City Mayfield
Company Wharton's Adirondack Outfitters
Contact Bill Wharton
City Lake Pleasant
Company White Dog Trail Company
Contact Jeff Whittemore
City Ilion

North Carolina

Company Buffalo Creek Guide Service
Contact Johnnie Dale
City Selma
Company Clear Creek Guest Ranch
Contact Rex Frederick
City Burnsville
Company Northampton Lodge
Contact Gene Varnadoe
City Seaboard

North Dakota

Company Central Flyway Outfitters
Contact Dean Kersten
City Kramer
Company Dakota Lodge & Trail Rides
Contact Loren V. Ross
City Medora
Company DNG Enterprise Guide Service
Contact David Garske
City Minnewaukan
Company Elkhom Lodge
Contact Jamie L. Wehrman
City Fortuna
Company Knife River Ranch Vacation
Contact Ronald P. Wanner
City Golden Valley
Company Little Knife Outfitters
Contact Glendon "Swede" Nelson
City Stanley
Company North Country Guide Service
Contact Rick (Richard) Darling
City Leeds
Company North Country Guiding
Contact Dawn Helwig Tim & Tom Mau
City Tolley
Company Northern Flight Guide Service
Contact Kyle Blanchfield
City Devils Lake
Company Northland Charter
Contact Larry Freed
City Bismarck
Company Red Willow Outfitters
Contact Jack Haines
City Wheatland
Company Spring Creek Guide Service
Contact Paul A. Olson
City Surrey
Company
Contact Marvin R. Dick
City Munich

Ohio

Company Chalets Newman-McKenzie
Contact
City Mainfield
Company Little River Lodge
Contact Chuck & Pat Crone
City West Miamisburg
Company T & T Outfitters
Contact Thomas Belville
City Proctorville

Oregon

Company Anderson Land & Livestock
Contact Terry Anderson
City Pilot Rock
Company Antlers Inn
Contact
City Ukiah
Company Bar M Dude Ranch
Contact The Baker Family
City Adams
Company Black Tails Unlimited
Contact John Lehnherr
City Jacksonville
Company Bob Spencer's McKenzie River Guide
Contact Bob Spencer
City Springfield
Company Brian Spangrud Professional Services
Contact Brian D. Spangrud
City Salem
Company C Bar C Outfitters
Contact Rocky Campbell
City Summerville
Company Cascade Adventures
Contact Darian Corey
City Sandy
Company Centerfire Outfitters
Contact Robert Rodgers
City Prineville
Company Central Coast Guide Service
Contact Mark Sehl
City Tidewater
Company Cornucopia Wilderness Pack Station
Contact Eldon & Marge Deardorff
City Richland
Company Cougar Creek Outfitter
Contact Foy Hopkins
City Joseph
Company Crazy Cayuse Ranch
Contact Ronald G. Adams
City Medford
Company Cyrus Happy Guide & Outfitter
Contact Cyrus Happy
City Portland
Company Dave's Guide Service
Contact David Johnson
City Jacksonville
Company Deadwood Outfitters
Contact Tom & Dawn Carter
City Baker City
Company Don's Guide Service
Contact Donald Hamblin
City Corvallis
Company Dusky Flyways
Contact Ronald Helgeson
City Rickreall
Company Elkhorn Guide Service
Contact Jeff Givens
City Redmond
Company Fir Mountain Ranch
Contact
City Hood River
Company Flying M Ranch
Contact Barbara & Bryce Mitchell
City Yamhill
Company Go West Outfitters
Contact Shawn Jones
City Prineville,
Company High Desert Outfitters
Contact Charles Messner
City Adel
Company Hurricane Creek Llama Treks, Inc.
Contact Stanlynn Daughterty
City Enterprise
Company James H. Arnold
Contact
City Salem
Company Lofton Creek Outfitters
Contact Brad Santucci
City Prineville
Company Lookout Outfitters
Contact Bill Zikmund
City Durkee
Company Magnum Adventures
Contact Blake D. Payne
City Springfield
Company Maverick Adventures
Contact Donald Dungey
City Medford
Company Moss Springs Packing
Contact Charlie Short
City Cove
Company Northwest Outdoor Specialties
Contact Donald Richelderfer
City Wasco
Company Outback Ranch Outfitters
Contact Jon & Tracie Wick
City Joseph
Company Paulina Tours
Contact Todd Brown
City La Pine
Company Real Eastern Oregon Tours
Contact Chary Mires
City Baker City
Company Rock Springs Guest Ranch
Contact
City Bend
Company Rouge River Guide Service
Contact Paul Lopes
City Grants Pass
Company S.A.L.E.M. Treks - Wiley Woods Ranch
Contact Kenneth W. Ploeser
City Salem
Company Sien's Guide Service
Contact Dale Siens
City Klamath Falls
Company Steens Mountain Packers
Contact John and Cindy Witzel
City Frenchglen
Company Stringham Outfitters, Inc.
Contact Steven L. Stringham
City Bend
Company The Oregon Experience

Contact Arden Corey
City Mill City
Company The Ultimate Llama
Contact Nancy J. Alderson
City Terrebonne
Company Tom Phillips Guide Service
Contact Tom Phillips
City Roseburg
Company Tri-State Outfitters
Contact Mark E. Moncrief
City Joseph
Company Up-A-Tree Guide Service
Contact Jason Gard
City Eugene
Company V & M Guide Service
Contact Vern Hayward
City Pendelton
Company Wallowa Llamas
Contact Raz & Louise Rasmussen and Steve Backstrom
City Halfway
Company Wapiti Outfitters
Contact Barbara Seeger
City Echo
Company Winema Outfitters
Contact Allan Vanzant
City Malin
Company
Contact Daniel M. Stucky
City Springfield

Pennsylvania

Company Arctic Outfitters
Contact Fred A. Webb & Sons
City Harleysville
Company Granite Creek Outfitters
Contact Jay King Jr.
City Wyommissing
Company Sylvania Tree Farm
Contact
City Lackawaxen

South Carolina

Company Barron Guide Service
Contact Henry Barron
City Laurens

South Dakota

Company Colony Outfitters
Contact Jim J. Dacar
City Belle Fourche
Company Gunsel Horse Adventure
Contact Robert D. Lantis
City Rapid City
Company Triple R Ranch
Contact
City Keystone
Company Willow Creek Wildlife Inc.
Contact Steve & Bob Stoeser
City Ft. Pierre

Texas

Company 50/50 Ranch
Contact Charles R. Carr
City San Antonio
Company AA Ranch
Contact Harry Wood
City Centerville
Company Adobe Lodge
Contact Skipper Duncan
City San Angelo
Company B. E. Wilson Corp.
Contact Michael Morris
City Del Rio
Company BACA Outfitters
Contact
City Abilene
Company Bajio Ranch
Contact Warren Uecker
City Fowlerton
Company Bald Eagle Ranch, Inc.
Contact
City Bandera
Company Brnovak
Contact Frank Brnovak
City Merkel
Company C Bar Land Cattle & Company
Contact Malcom Calaway
City Alpine
Company C.R. Baker Ranch
Contact Hazel E. Johnson
City Burnet
Company Canyon Springs Ranch/Texas Exotic Safaris
Contact Frank Pulkrabek
City Ingram
Company Carleton Ranches
Contact J. Preston Carleton
City Cedar Park
Company Circle "E" Ranch
Contact
City Dallas
Company Cohen Ranch
Contact Opal & Bob Cohen
City Marble Falls
Company Crene Ranch Company
Contact E. J. or Jimmy Crane
City Del Rio
Company Cutbirth Cattle Company, LTD
Contact Kyle Cutbirth
City Brownwood
Company Dochada
Contact Charles E. Bearden
City Wichita Falls
Company Double T Ranch
Contact Tim & Trudy Schmidt
City Mason
Company Dunbar Ranch
Contact Dayn Dunbar
City Junction
Company Emzy Barker Outfitters
Contact
City Taylor
Company Farmland
Contact Eddie Earl Shaw Jr.
City Houston
Company Ford Ranch
Contact
City Melvin
Company Fort McKavett Outfitters
Contact Jimmy Cahill
City Sonora
Company Foster & Foster Ranch
Contact J. L. & M. K. Foster
City Friendswood
Company Four Arrows Outfitters
Contact Jarred Peeples
City San Antonio
Company Frantzen Ranch
Contact Henry Frantzen
City Fredericksburg
Company Hagerman Ranch
Contact Kenneth Dolezalek
City Sherman
Company Harvester Hill Ranch
Contact Stephanie Burman
City Hockley
Company Homer Martin Ranch
Contact Homer Martin Jr.
City Mason
Company Inks Ranch
Contact Jin Inks
City Llano
Company Irvin Ranch
Contact Larry Irvin
City Abilene
Company J.T. Maner Ranch
Contact
City Harper
Company Jarrett Juno Ranch
Contact Norman Farmer
City Comstock
Company Jennings Ranch
Contact Gary Jennings
City Fredonia
Company Kash Ranch
Contact Karl Kash
City Kerrville
Company Kuykendall Ranch
Contact Dale Perry
City Cherokee
Company Lee Phillips Ranch
Contact Lee Phillips
City Austin
Company Leon Harrel's Old West Adventure
Contact
City Kerrville
Company Lone Star Trail Outfitters
Contact Trent Huckaby
City Ft. Stockton
Company Mauldins Place/Griswald Ranch
Contact Mr. & Mrs. C. W. Mauldin
City Gordon
Company Mesa Ranch
Contact E. G. Nava

City Hebbroville
Company Nail Ranch
Contact Craig Winters
City Albany
Company Operation Orphans
Contact
City Mason
Company Pila Blanca Ranch
Contact Jesse M. Ruiz
City San Antonio
Company Ponderosa R Ranch
Contact Orville & Rebecca Luedecke
City Eden
Company Proffitt's Farm & Ranch
Contact Kenneth Proffitt
City Austin
Company R.E. Jackson Ranch - Resort #1
Contact
City Cleveland
Company Rafter W Ranches
Contact Jack Wardlaw
City Sonora
Company Red Bluff Ranch
Contact Dalton L. Bowere
City Bangs
Company Ricardo Ranch
Contact Bobby Hill
City Fairfield
Company Riggs Ranch
Contact Teddy R. Riggs Jr.
City Pearsall
Company Robby Robinson Ranches
Contact Robby Robinson
City Junction
Company Rock Eagle Ranch Corp.
Contact Richard E. Weinberg
City Bellaire
Company Rockin' B Ranch
Contact Aubrey L. Brown
City Del Rio
Company Rocky Top Outfitters
Contact Rudy Steele
City Wylie
Company Running-R Guest Ranch, Inc.
Contact Ralph & Iris Kirchner & Charles "Doo" Robbins
City Bandera
Company Santa Catalina Ranch
Contact G. Sisco
City San Antonio
Company Stovall Ranch
Contact Eric Martin Stovall
City Marathon
Company Sycamore Ranch
Contact Wilson Hodge
City Del Rio
Company Thompson Temple's Texas Wildlife
Contact Thompson Temple
City Ingram
Company Triangle T Outfitters
Contact Ed James Tibljas
City Granbury
Company Wendel Ranch
Contact Lorenz or Jannabeth Wendel
City Fredericksburg
Company West Outfitters
Contact Ronnie West
City Winnsboro
Company Williams Ranch Co.
Contact Rowdy McBride
City Alpine

Utah

Company All 'Round Ranch
Contact
City Jensen
Company Black Mountain Outfitters
Contact
City Panguitch
Company Buffalo Pointe, Inc.
Contact
City Syracuse
Company Chapoose Rivers & Trails
Contact
City Fort Duchesne
Company Cougar Country Outfitters & Guide Service
Contact Karen Lacunate
City New Harmony
Company Cowboy Trails
Contact
City Moab
Company Cowpie Backcountry Adventures
Contact
City Magna
Company Coyote Road
Contact
City Draper
Company Dalton Gang Adventures
Contact
City Monticello
Company Ed Black Trail Rides
Contact
City Monument Valley
Company Johnson Cattle Company
Contact
City Aurora
Company Ken Sleight Pack Trips
Contact Ken Sleight
City Moab
Company La Gracious Stables
Contact
City Rockville
Company Monument Valley Trail Rides
Contact
City Mexican Hat
Company Navajo County Guided Trail Rides
Contact
City Monument Valley
Company Nine Mile Ranch
Contact
City Wellington
Company Outlaw Trails, Inc.
Contact
City Hanksville
Company Pack Creek Ranch
Contact
City Moab
Company Pack Saddle Trips
Contact
City Hurricane
Company Quarter Circle E Guest Ranch
Contact
City LaPoint
Company Red Rock Adventure
Contact
City Tropic
Company Redd Ranches
Contact David Redd
City La Sal
Company Reid Ranch
Contact
City Salt Lake City
Company Rock Creek Guest Ranch/ Flying J Outfitters
Contact Lawny Jackson-Manager
City Myton
Company Rock Creek Ranch
Contact
City Price
Company Rock Creek Ranch, Corp.
Contact
City Mountain Home
Company Rocking "R" Ranch
Contact
City Provo
Company Rocky C Adventures
Contact
City Ogden
Company Rocky Meadow Adventures
Contact
City Bluebell
Company Rosebud Llamas Utah
Contact Shirley Weathers & Bill Walsh
City Fruitland
Company Ruby Ranch
Contact
City Green River
Company Ruby's Outlaw Trail Rides
Contact
City Bryce
Company San Rafael Trail Rides
Contact
City Elmo
Company Scenic Rim Trail Rides
Contact
City Tropic
Company Scenic Safaris
Contact
City Cannonville
Company Tanner Ranch
Contact
City Orangeville
Company The Alternate Transit Authority
Contact
City Draper
Company Totem Pole Tours & Trailrides
Contact
City Monument Valley
Company Utah Escapades
Contact
City Park City
Company Zion's Kolob Mountain Ranch
Contact
City Provo
Company Zion's Ponderosa Resort

Contact
City Salt Lake City

Vermont

Company All About Trout
Contact Erik Bleckner & Scott Bevill
City Burlington
Company Firefly Ranch
Contact Marie Louise Link
City Bristol
Company Green Mountain Long Beards
Contact Michael C. Senecal
City Manchester Ctr.
Company Green Mtn. Outdoor Adv./ Ridge Runner Bowhunts
Contact James or Sharon Paige
City Montpelier
Company Hubbard Park Outfitters
Contact John Guilmette
City Waterbury
Company Otter Creek Outfitters
Contact Daniel Barrows
City Vergennes
Company Seymour Lake Lodge
Contact Dave or Sue Benware
City Morgan
Company The Outside Connection
Contact Bryce M. Towsley
City East Clarendon
Company Thurston's Guide Service
Contact Sidney F. Thurston
City Waterbury Ctr.
Company Vermont Icelandic Horse Farm
Contact
City Waitsfield
Company Willoughby Lodge Enterprises
Contact Malcolm Davidson Sr.
City Springfield

Washington

Company Back Country Wilderness Outfitters
Contact Dave Porter & Jim McWorter
City Longview
Company Bobcat Ranch
Contact
City Wasjpiga
Company Cascade Wilderness Outfitters
Contact Steve Darwood
City Carlton
Company Cusack's Alaska Lodge
Contact Master Guide Bob Cusack
City Mercer Island
Company Eagle Tours
Contact Charles W. Baldwin
City Vancouver
Company Early Winters Outfitting
Contact Aaron Lee & Judy Burkhart
City Mazama
Company High Country Outfitters/Camp Wahoo
Contact Debby Miller
City Issaquah
Company Indian Creek Corral
Contact Dan & Carleen Bleton
City Naches
Company K Diamond K Ranch
Contact
City Republic
Company Panhandle Outfitters
Contact Tom Loder
City Valleyford
Company Selkirk G&O/Priest Lk. Outdoor Adv.
Contact Patrick J. Prentice & Bruce Duncan
City Newman Lake
Company Susee's Skyline Packers
Contact Albert L. "Roy" Susee
City Tacoma
Company Vail's Guide Service
Contact Bob Vail
City McCleary

West Virginia

Company Cheat Mtn. Outfitting & Guide Service
Contact Treve Painter
City Durbin
Company Greenbrier River Company
Contact Virgil Hanshaw
City Ronceverte
Company Madd Jack Trading Post and Campground
Contact Jack and Jackie Clark
City Ramsey
Company Moutaineer Guides
Contact Richard T. Shepherd
City Fairmont
Company New/Gauley Expeditions, Inc.
Contact Keith Spangler
City Lansing

Wisconsin

Company Alpine House Country Chalet
Contact
City Cashton
Company Argosy Adventures Whitewater Raft Co.
Contact
City Niagara
Company Blue Diamond Whitetail Ranch
Contact David Zirbel
City Gaysmill
Company Bridger Peak Outfitters LLC
Contact Robert Millar
City Stoughton
Company Chip's Call of the Wild Guide Service
Contact Chip Mosser
City Merrill
Company Country Gardens
Contact
City Egg Harbor
Company Dorset Ridge Guest House
Contact
City Wilton
Company Double K-D Ranch
Contact
City Baraboo
Company East Shore Inn
Contact
City Chilton
Company Ethilton Farms
Contact
City Hartford
Company Foster Farmhouse Vacation Home
Contact Mr. Williamson
City Porterfield
Company Grady's Farm Bed & Breakfast
Contact
City Portage
Company Herb's Wolf River Whitewater Rafting
Contact
City White Lake
Company Hickory Lane Farm
Contact
City Cambridge
Company Hoppe Homestead, Since 1866
Contact
City East Troy
Company Hunky Dory Farm Resort
Contact
City Balsam Lake
Company Just-N-Trails Bed & Breakfast
Contact
City Sparta
Company Little House on the Kickapoo
Contact
City LaFarge
Company Lonesome Jake's Devil's Hole Ranch
Contact
City Norwalk
Company Mother Earth Lodge
Contact
City Elton
Company Pinehaven Bed & Breakfast
Contact
City Baraboo
Company Red Bud Country Inn
Contact
City Wausau
Company Ridge Runner Outfitters
Contact Tom Haack
City Sheboygan
Company River Ridge Stock & Fiber Farm
Contact
City Bruce
Company Sturgeon Lake Lodge
Contact Shannono & Don Utynek
City Beloit
Company Thunder Valley Bed &

Breakfast
Contact
City Wisconsin Dells
Company Timberidge
Contact
City Madison
Company Trail Farm
Contact
City Westboro
Company Trail-Side Bed 'n Breakfast
Contact
City Wilton
Company Trillium
Contact
City LaFarge
Company Tuck-A-Way Camp
Contact
City North Freedom
Company Wolfway Farm
Contact
City West Salem
Company Woodside Ranch Resort
Contact
City Mauston

Wyoming

Company 46 Outfitters
Contact R. Lane Turner
City Shoshoni
Company 7D Ranch
Contact Marshall Dominick
City Cody
Company 88 Ranch Outfitters
Contact William Henry III/Robert Henry
City Douglas
Company AA Outfitters
Contact Ronald Ball
City Big Piney
Company Absaroka Mountain Lodge
Contact Bob Kudelski
City Cody
Company Absaroka Mountain Lodge Resort
Contact Dave & Cathy Sweet
City Wapiti
Company Absaroka Ranch
Contact Budd Betts
City Dubois
Company AJ Brink Outfitters
Contact Jim Brink
City Jelm
Company AJ Outfitters
Contact Jeffery HIll
City Casper
Company Aladdin Outfitters
Contact Walter Marchant
City Aladdin
Company All American Outfitters
Contact Forest Stearns
City Wilson
Company Allen's Diamond Four Wilderness Ranch
Contact Jim Allen
City Lander
Company Antelope Outfitters
Contact Steve Beilgard
City Buffalo
Company Arizona Creek Outfitters
Contact Roy Bonner
City Jackson
Company Arrowhead Outfitters
Contact Bobby Lowe
City Jackson Hole
Company Aspen Grove Ranch Outfittters
Contact Frederick Neuman
City Rawlins
Company Autumn Meadows
Contact Gary Dean Buck
City Encampment
Company B & B Outfitters
Contact Brett Jones
City Thermopolis
Company B.J. Outfitters
Contact James Ellison
City Casper
Company Bar Diamond R Outfitters
Contact Brad & Van Dana
City Thayne
Company Bar-J Ranch
Contact
City Wilson
Company Barlow Outfitting/Fort Jackson River Trips
Contact Robert L. Barlow
City Alpine
Company BB Outfitters
Contact Brian Beishers
City Sheridan
Company Bear Lodge Outfitters
Contact Kenneth Rathbun
City Sundance
Company Beard Outfitters
Contact Lyle Beard
City Tetonia
Company Beartooth & Absaroka Wilderness
Contact Charles H. Smith
City Cody
Company Beaver Creek Outfitters
Contact Steve Kobold
City Sheridan
Company Beaver Creek Outfitters
Contact L.D.Gibertz
City Gillette
Company Beaver Trap Outfitters
Contact Al Martin
City Dayton
Company Big Horn Basin Outfitters
Contact Ed R. Cormier
City Worland
Company Big Horn Outfitters
Contact John Nation
City Lovell
Company Bitterroot Ranch
Contact Bayard Fox
City Dubois
Company BJ Outfitters
Contact William Hollingsworth
City Casper
Company Blackwater Creek Ranch
Contact Tom & Debbie Carlton
City Cody
Company Bolten Ranch Outfitters
Contact Robert Terrill
City Cheyenne
Company Boulder Lake Lodge
Contact Kim Bright
City Pinedale
Company Box K Ranch
Contact Walter Korn
City Moran
Company Boysen Outfitters
Contact William M. Weaver
City Thermopolis
Company Broken Horn Outfitters
Contact Rock Buckingham
City Kaycee
Company Brooks Lake Lodge
Contact Will Rigsby
City Dubois
Company Brush Creek Guest Ranch
Contact
City Saratoga
Company Buckhorn Mountain Outfitters
Contact Jerry Martin
City Dayton
Company Buffalo Creek Outfitters
Contact Otis Bloom
City Evansville
Company Butte Creek Outfitters
Contact Theresa Lineberger
City Cody
Company C Bar C Outfitters
Contact Clifford J. Clark
City Casper
Company Cabin Creek Outfitters
Contact Duane Wiltse
City Cody
Company Cash Outfitters
Contact Douglas Cash
City Kaycee
Company Castle Rock Ranch
Contact
City Cody
Company Cherokee Outfitters
Contact Ivan L. Samson
City Fort Laramie
Company Cody's Ranch Resort
Contact Barbara Cody
City Cody
Company Cole Creek Outfitters
Contact Jon C. Nicolaysen
City Casper
Company Cow Camp
Contact
City Recluse
Company Cowboy Village Resort
Contact
City Moran
Company Cowpoke Outfitters
Contact Jack Risner
City Baggs
Company Crandall Creek Outfitters
Contact Bruce Hillard
City Casper
Company Cross C Ranch & Outfitting
Contact Willard M. Woods
City Wheatland
Company D & D Outfitters

Contact
City Worland
Company Dampier Hunting Lodge
Contact James Dampier
City Newcastle
Company Dan Kinneman Outfitter-Guide
Contact Daniel Kinneman
City Dubois
Company Darby Mountain Outfitters
Contact R. John Harper and Chuck Thornton
City Big Piney
Company Darwin Ranch
Contact Loring Woodman
City Jackson
Company Dave Filtner Packing & Outfitting
Contact David Filtner
City Greybull
Company Dave Hanna Outfitters
Contact Dave Hanna
City Jackson
Company David Ranch
Contact Melvin David
City Daniel
Company Deadman Creek Outfitters
Contact Gregg Fischer
City Alpine
Company Deer Forks Ranch
Contact Benny Middleton
City Douglas
Company Diamond D Ranch Outfitters
Contact Rod Doty
City Moran
Company Diamond Tail Outfitters
Contact Stan Filtner
City Greybull
Company Dick Page
Contact Richard L. Page
City Casper
Company Don (Tip) Tipton's Outfitting
Contact Don K. Tipton
City Casper
Company Don Scheer Outfitters
Contact Don Scheer
City Dubois
Company Double Diamond Outfitters
Contact Reed "Rick" Miller
City Afton
Company Double Diamond Outfitters
Contact Craig Griffith
City Meeteetse
Company Double Diamond X Ranch
Contact Dale Sims, Jr.
City Cody
Company Dunior Outfitters Corp.
Contact George William Snodgrass
City Dubois
Company Early Guest Ranch
Contact Ruth & Wayne Campbell
City Crowheart
Company Eatons Ranch
Contact
City Wolf
Company Elephant Head Lodge
Contact Phil & Joan Lamb
City Wapiti
Company Elk Antler Outfitters
Contact Richard Ashburn
City Jackson
Company Elk Mountain Outfitters
Contact Myron J. Wakkuri
City Wheatland
Company Even Toe Outfitters
Contact Phil Gonzales
City Buffalo
Company Flying B Outfitters
Contact Bill Gauger
City Casper
Company Flying H Ranch
Contact John and Amee Barrus
City Cody
Company Flying S Outfitters
Contact Kathleen M. Steele
City Aladdin
Company Flying U Ranch
Contact Ralph Foster
City Claremont
Company Flying W Horse Service, Inc.
Contact Gordon C. White
City Thayne
Company Flying X Ranch
Contact Earl (Sonny) Malley
City Wheatland
Company Forest Dell Guest Ranch
Contact Low & Ads Mae Gardner
City Smoot
Company Gary Fales Outfitting
Contact Gary Fales
City Cody
Company General Outfitter
Contact Ronald O. Titterington
City Dubois
Company Grand and Sierra Outfitter
Contact Glen Knotwell & Skyler Knotwell
City Encampment
Company Granstorm Outfitters
Contact Swede Granstorm
City Buffalo
Company Grassy Lake Outfitters
Contact Dan Blair
City Afton
Company Greer Outfitters
Contact Randy & Lora Greer
City Gillette
Company Grizzly Outfitters
Contact Cole & Elaine Benton
City Buffalo
Company Gros Ventre River Ranch
Contact
City Moose
Company Hart Brothers Partnership
Contact William Hart
City Dubois
Company Hayden & Sons Ranch
Contact Troy Hayden
City Gillette
Company Hensley Trophy Outfitter
Contact Rob Hensley
City Casper
Company Hidden Basin Outfitters
Contact Phillip & George Engler
City Jackson
Company Hidden Creek Outfitters
Contact Bill Perry
City Cody
Company Hidden Valley Ranch
Contact Duaine & Sheila Hagen
City Cody
Company High Island Ranch & Cattle Co.
Contact Karen Robbins
City Hamilton Dome
Company Highland Meadow Outfitters
Contact Mark Thompson
City Dubois
Company Hiland Outfitters
Contact Don Bennett
City Hiland
Company Horse Creek Land Co.
Contact Kenneth Neal
City Dubois
Company Hunton Creek Outfitters
Contact Clark Noble
City Wheatland
Company Indian Creek Outfitters
Contact Bruce & Angela Moyer
City Jackson
Company Indian Summer Outfitters
Contact Steve Robertson
City Jackson
Company Ishawooa Outfitters
Contact Monte Horst
City Cody
Company J & B Outfitters
Contact Jim Fritz
City Casper
Company Jackson Hole Mountain Guides
Contact Andy Carson
City Jackson
Company Jenkins Hunting Camp
Contact Larry Jenkins
City Freedom
Company Jiggs Pack & Guide Service
Contact Jiggs Black
City Riverton
Company John Henry Lee Outfitters, Inc.
Contact John Lee
City Jackson
Company Johnson's A Bar One Ranch
Contact Clyde Johnson
City Elk Mountain
Company Jones Outfitters
Contact Patrick Jones
City Laramie
Company K Bar Outfitting
Contact John Buxton II
City Laramie
Company K Bar Z Guest Ranch & Outfitters
Contact Dave Segall and Dawna Barnett
City Cody
Company Kedesh Guest Ranch
Contact Charles Lander
City Shell
Company Lander Llama Company
Contact Scott Woodruff
City Lander
Company Laramie Range Outfitters
Contact John Bisbing
City Douglas

Company Larry Stetter, General Outfitter
Contact Larry Stetter
City Dubois
Company Lazy BJ Outfitters
Contact Bill Woodworth
City Gillette
Company Lazy L & B Ranch
Contact Lee & Bob Naylon
City Dubois
Company Lee Livingston Outfitting
Contact Lee Livingston
City Cody
Company Let's Gallop Horseback Adventures/Sandy Gap Ranch
Contact Frank Deede & Kerry Thomas
City Pinedale
Company Lightning Creek Ranch
Contact Jim Werner
City Douglas
Company Linn Brothers Outfitting
Contact Eugene Linn
City Wilson
Company Little Sunlight Outfitters
Contact Don J. Vitto
City Hulett
Company Llano Outfitters
Contact John F. Savini
City Casper
Company Lone Wolf Outfitters
Contact Bambi Schumacher
City Buffalo
Company Lost Creek Outfitters
Contact Ron & Kathi Clark
City Thayne
Company Lost Creek Ranch Resorts
Contact Mike & Bev Halpin
City Moose
Company Lozier's Box "R" Ranch
Contact Levi M. Lozier
City Cora
Company M & M Outfitters
Contact Mark K. Teel
City Gillette
Company Majo Ranch
Contact Grant Stambaugh
City Cody
Company Mangis Guide Service
Contact Klay Mangis
City Jackson
Company Mankin Wildlife
Contact James R. Mankin
City Gillette
Company McNell & Sons
Contact Merrill McNell
City Alpine
Company Medicine Bow Outfitters
Contact Harold Embree
City Medicine Bow
Company Mike Smith Outfitters
Contact Michael Smith
City Shell
Company Mill Iron Ranch
Contact Chancy Wheeldon
City Jackson
Company Moose Head Ranch
Contact
City Moose
Company Nelson Outfitting
Contact David & Dennis Nelson
City Sheridan
Company North Fork Outfitters
Contact Jim VanNorman
City Edgerton
Company North Laramie Outfitting & Guide
Contact Allen L. Cook
City Wheatland
Company North Rim Outfitters
Contact Roy Gamblin
City Wheatland
Company Northern Wyoming Outfitters
Contact George K. Warner
City Sheridan
Company NX Bar Ranch
Contact Brian MacCarty
City Sheridan
Company Old Glendevey Ranch
Contact Garth W. Peterson
City Jelm
Company Open Creek Outfitting
Contact John Billings
City Cody
Company P Cross Bar Ranch
Contact Marion & Mary Scott
City Gillette
Company Pahaska Tepee
Contact Bob Coe
City Cody
Company Paintrock Adventures, LLC
Contact Todd Jones
City Hyattville
Company Paintrock Outfitters
Contact William F. Craft
City Greybull
Company Papoose Peak Outfitters
Contact Louis Cary
City Cody
Company Paradise Ranch Co.
Contact James Anderson
City Buffalo
Company Pass Creek Outfitters
Contact Richard Miller
City Arapahoe
Company Pat Garrett Outfitter
Contact Pat Garrett
City Kaycee
Company Pennoyer Outfitting
Contact George Pennoyer
City Thermopolis
Company Peterson's Hunting Camps
Contact Everett D. & Pat Peterson
City Afton
Company Pine Creek Outfitters
Contact Earl Wright
City Big Piney
Company Piney Creek Outfitters
Contact Ron Reece
City Story
Company Powder Horn Outfitters
Contact Darwin Powers
City Ranchester
Company Powder River Breaks Outfitters
Contact Glenn Sorenson
City Arvada
Company Powder River Outfitters
Contact John Francis
City Buffalo
Company Pronghorn Adventures
Contact Greg Salisbury
City Encampment
Company Pumpkin Buttes Outfitters
Contact Bill Bruce Hines
City Gillette
Company R Lazy S Ranch
Contact Bob & CLaire McConaughty
City Teton Village
Company R.E. Evans Grizzly Creek Outfitters
Contact Richard Evans
City Cody
Company Rafter B Outfitters
Contact Larry Brannian
City Buffalo
Company Rand Creek Outfitters
Contact Ron McCloud
City Cody
Company Rand Creek Ranch
Contact Kevin & Darlene Lauer
City Wapiti
Company Ranger Creek Ranch
Contact Claude A. Powell
City Dayton
Company Red Cloud Outfitting
Contact Brett L. Sorenson
City Story
Company Red Desert Outfitters
Contact Vic Dana
City Rock Springs
Company Red Rock Ranch
Contact
City Kelly
Company Red Valley Outfitters
Contact Mike Wolcott
City Kaycee
Company Rendezvous Outfitters
Contact Bruce Blanthorn
City Bondurant
Company Rewah Ranch
Contact Pete Kunz
City Jelm
Company Ridgemaster Outfitting
Contact Charles Cureton
City Casper
Company Rimrock Ranch
Contact Glenn Fales
City Cody
Company Rocking L-H
Contact Larry J. Henry
City Bondurant
Company Rocky Butte Outfitters
Contact Ed G. Schaffer
City Gillette
Company Romios Outfitters
Contact Pete Romios
City Encampment
Company Ron Dube's Wilderness Adv.
Contact Ron & Carol Dube
City Wapiti
Company Ronell Skinner Guide & Outfitters
Contact Ronell Skinner
City Bedford
Company Rough Country Outfitters &

Guides
Contact James D. Schell
City Glenrock
Company Sagebrush Outfitters
Contact Don Hockett
City Gillette
Company Savage Run Outfitters
Contact James F. Talbott
City Laramie
Company Schively Ranch
Contact
City Lovell
Company Schmalz Outfitting
Contact Don & Patti Jo Schmalz
City Cody
Company Seven D Ranch
Contact Nikki & Marshall Dominick I. Ward
City Cody
Company Seven J Outfitters
Contact Jeffery L. Smith
City Sundance
Company Sheep Mesa Outfitters
Contact Ronald Good
City Cody
Company Sheep Mountain Outfitters
Contact Tim Haberberger
City Alpine
Company Shirley Mountain Outfitters
Contact Steve Steinle
City Mills
Company Shoal Creek Outfitters
Contact Scott Millward
City Jackson
Company Shoshone Lodge Outfitters & Guest Ranch
Contact Keith Dahlem
City Cody
Company Sleeping Indian Outfitters
Contact Paul Crittenden
City Bondurant
Company Snake River Outfitters
Contact Thomas Grieve
City Baggs
Company SNS Outfitters & Guide Service
Contact SY Gilliland
City Casper
Company Snyder Outfitting
Contact Stanley Snyder
City Big Horn
Company Southern Wyoming Outfitters
Contact Dale Pribyl
City Laramie
Company Spear-O-Wigwam Ranch
Contact James Niner
City Sheridan
Company Spearhead Ranch
Contact Frank N. Moore
City Douglas
Company Squaw Creek Ranch & Outfitters
Contact Gail Zimmerman
City Cody
Company Star Valley Outfitters
Contact Reed S. Clark
City Afton
Company Steve Sheaffer Outfitters
Contact Steve & Connie Sheaffer
City Laramie
Company Suda Outfitters
Contact Wayne Suda
City Dubois
Company Sully Outfitters
Contact Sully Simons
City Beulah
Company Sunrise Outfitters
Contact Mike Heins
City Gillette
Company Sweetwater Fishing Expeditions
Contact George H. Hunker
City Lander
Company Sweetwater Gap Ranch
Contact Robert Wilmetti
City Rock Springs
Company Sweetwater Outfitters
Contact Ray A. Dennis
City Casper
Company Swift Creek Outfitters
Contact B.J. & Vicki Hill
City Afton
Company Swift Creek Outfitters
Contact Therese Metherell
City Jackson
Company T Cross Ranch
Contact Ken & Garey Neal
City Dubois
Company T Lazy T Outfitters
Contact Tom Toolson
City Jackson
Company Table Mountain Outfitters
Contact Dale Critchfield
City Cheyenne
Company Tally-Ho Outfitters
Contact Allan Perry
City Kaycee
Company Taylor Outfitters
Contact Tory Taylor
City Dubois
Company Taylor Ranch & Outfitting
Contact Glenn B. Taylor
City Kelly
Company Teton Crest Outfitters
Contact Phil Major
City Wilson
Company Teton Wilderness Outfitting
Contact Nate C. Vance
City Cody
Company The Beartree Brand Range Riders
Contact Roger & Bonnie Preston
City Bedford
Company The Head Hunters
Contact Don C. Malli
City Arvada
Company The Hideout, Flitner Ranch
Contact Kathryn Flitner
City Greybull
Company The Last Resort
Contact Dru Roberts
City Daniel
Company Thompson Outfitters
Contact Dick Thompson
City Cora
Company Thunder Ridge Outfitters
Contact Ron Morrison
City Casper
Company Timber Creek Outfitters
Contact Tim Hockhalter
City Cody
Company Tracker, Packer & Guide Outfitting
Contact Gary Dean Talbott
City Encampment
Company Trail Creek Ranch
Contact Elizabeth Woolsey & Alexandra Grant
City Wilson
Company Trails West Outfitters
Contact Robert Sundeen
City Buffalo
Company Trefren Outfitters
Contact Tim & Sharon Trefren
City Thayne
Company Triangle C Ranch
Contact The Garnick Family
City Dubois
Company Triangle X Ranch
Contact John Turner
City Moose
Company Triple Three Outfitters
Contact J. Craig Smith
City Buffalo
Company Two Bars Seven Ranch
Contact
City Tie Siding
Company Two Ocean Pass Outfitting
Contact John R. Winter
City Moran
Company UL Ranch Outfitters
Contact Jerry R. Palm
City Elk Mountain
Company Ullery Outfitters
Contact Brad Ullery
City Casper
Company V Bar F Cattle Co.
Contact Neal R. Schuman
City Buffalo
Company Wade's Piney Creek Outfitting
Contact Bobbi Wade
City Big Piney
Company Wayne Graves Outfitters
Contact Wayne Graves
City Kaycee
Company Whiskey Mountain Outfitters
Contact Gari Epp
City Dubois
Company Whitetail Creek Outfitters
Contact Raymond M. Hulse
City Hulett
Company Wildcat Outfitters
Contact Pat Phillipps
City Douglas
Company Wilderness Trails
Contact Galloway M. Clover
City Jackson
Company Wind River Mountain Outfitters
Contact Fritz Meyer
City Dubois
Company Wind River Outfitters
Contact Kim Merchant
City Evansville
Company Windy Peak Outfitters

Contact Darin Geringer
City Glendo
Company Wolf Lake Outfitters
Contact Mike Nystrom
City Pinedale
Company Wolverine Creek Outfitters
Contact Warren Fleming
City Jackson
Company Wyoming Country Outfitters
Contact Kevin McNiven
City Lander
Company Wyoming Dark Timber Adv.
Contact Dave Parrish
City Green River
Company Wyoming Peak Outfitters
Contact
City Afton
Company Wyoming's Choice
Contact Dick Vandeveer
City Casper
Company Yellowstone Outfitters
Contact Gary Caskey
City Pinedale
Company ZN Outfitters
Contact George Williams
City Saratoga

Canada

Alberta

Company Alberta Bush Adventures
Contact Richard Deslauriers
City McLennan
Company Alberta Frontier Wilderness Adventures
Contact Judy & Ed Walker
City Sundre
Company Alberta Native Guide Service
Contact Ken Steinhauer
City Edmonton
Company Alberta Rocky Mountain Trail Adv.
Contact K&M Robinson & L&M Nielson
City Del Bonita
Company Alberta Wilderness Guide Service
Contact David Bzawy & Terry Birkholz
City Edmonton
Company All-Terrain Guide & Outfitting
Contact Ronald Bell
City Edmonton
Company Alstott Outfitting
Contact Edwin Alstott
City Caroline
Company Andrew Lake Lodge & Camp
Contact Glen Wettlaufer
City Edmonton
Company Athabasca River Outfitters
Contact Bryan Radke & Bruce Wierenga
City Barrhead
Company Barrier Mountain Outfitters
Contact A. H. Johnson
City Olds
Company Bearpaw Outfitting
Contact Scott Taylor
City St. Isidore
Company Big Rack Adventures
Contact Blair & Kathy Trout
City Newbrook
Company Big Smoky Outfitting, Ltd.
Contact Gary & Ricki Kruger
City Westlock
Company Blue Bronna Guiding & Outfitting
Contact Glenn Brown
City Three Hills
Company Blue Ridge Outfitters
Contact Wynder & Billl Barrus Dee
City Cardston
Company Boss Guiding Services
Contact Bob Byers
City Stettler
Company Brewster Mountain Packtrain
Contact
City Banff
Company Broadhead Outfitters
Contact Kent Butterfield
City Stettler
Company Chester Sands Outfitting
Contact Chester Sands
City Rocky Mountain House
Company Chimney Creek Outfitters
Contact Miles & Joanne Stern
City Edson
Company Cook & Sands Ranch
Contact Bill Sand & Sons
City Valleyview
Company Cypress Expeditions
Contact Lyle Czember
City Medicine Hat
Company D & S Guiding
Contact Robert Dean Cumming
City Viking
Company DeBolt Guiding & Outfitting
Contact Hugh Alexander
City Gibbons
Company Diamond And-A-Half Outfitters
Contact Bill Sinclair
City Wembley
Company Diamond Outfitters
Contact Byron Tofteland
City Valhalla Centre
Company Double Diamond Outfitters
Contact Gordon Burton
City Okotoks
Company Elk Island Outfitters
Contact Bernd Light
City Fort Saskatchewan
Company Eric's Wilderness
Contact Eric Twardzilk
City Edmonton
Company Excell Outfitters
Contact Al Schulz
City Westlock
Company Folding Mountain Outfitters
Contact Dale Drinkall
City Stavely
Company Frank Kuhnen
Contact Frank Kuhnen
City Red Deer
Company George Kelly Outfitters
Contact George Kelly
City Hinton
Company Glacier Peak Adventures
Contact Nancy Koopman
City Beaverlodge
Company Goffitt River Outfitters
Contact Rod E. Roth
City Manning
Company Golden Bear Outfitting
Contact Eldon Hoff
City Standard
Company Great North Outfitters
Contact Neil Wunderlich
City Edmonton
Company Great White Holdings
Contact Lloyd McMahon
City Lloydminster
Company Grizzly Trail Guiding & Outfitting
Contact Leo Schmaus
City Barrhead
Company Grosso Outfitting
Contact Clayton & Hilda Grosso
City Rocky Mountain House
Company Guinn Outfitters
Contact Rick & Denise Guinn
City Kananaskis Village Resort
Company Gundahoo River Outfitters
Contact Art Thompson
City Caroline
Company Hebert's Guide Service
Contact Joe & Doreen Hebert
City Valleyview
Company Homeplace Ranch
Contact Mac Makenny
City Priddis
Company Horseback Adventures Ltd.
Contact Tom Vinson
City Brule
Company J.W. & Edith Nagy Outfitting
Contact J.W. & Edith Nagy
City Didsbury
Company Jack Franklin Outfitting
Contact
City Brooks
Company JH Trail Rides
Contact Del Whitford
City Caroline
Company Jim Fisher Guiding & Outfitting
Contact Jim Fisher
City Rocky Mountain House
Company Jordy McAuley Outfitting
Contact Jordy McAuley
City Fairview
Company K Country Outfitting
Contact Keith Koebisch
City Cochrane
Company Kevin Rolfe Outfitters
Contact Kevin Rolfe
City Edmonton
Company Kostynuk Outfitting
Contact Sam Kostynuk

City Rocky Mountain House
Company Lazy H Trail Co.
Contact Richard & Connie Blair
City Cochrane
Company Leonard Outfitting
Contact Bazil Leonard
City Grand Cache
Company Lost Guide Outfitters
Contact Gary Bracken
City Sundre
Company McKenzie Brothers Outfitting
Contact Bruce & Linda McKenzie
City Edmonton
Company N.W.T. Outfitters
Contact Darrell & Duane Nelson
City Glenwood
Company North River Outfitting
Contact Ron Nemetchek
City Sherwood Park
Company Northern Adventures
Contact Pat Frederick
City Edmonton
Company Outlaws Guiding & Outfitting
Contact Frank Raymond
City Sundre
Company Plihal Guiding & Outffiting
Contact Gene Plihal
City Falher
Company Porcupine Creek Outfitters
Contact Brent Sinclair
City Pincher Creek
Company Raven Outfitters
Contact Wayne Whitherspoon
City Edmonton
Company Ray Cross & Sons Outfitting
Contact Ray W. Cross
City Fort Assiniboine
Company Rocking Star Trail Rides
Contact Willie Kadatz
City Rocky Mountain House
Company Ryk Visscher Bowhunting Adventures
Contact Ryk Visscher
City Edmonton
Company Sands & Miller Outfitting
Contact Don Miller & Charlie Sands
City Rocky Mountain House
Company Sheep Creek Outfitters
Contact Frank Simpson
City Claresholm
Company Sherwood Guides & Outfitters
Contact Lois or Pete McMann
City Sherwood Park
Company Silver Fox Outfitters
Contact Eric Rauhanen
City Medley
Company Silver Sage Outfitters
Contact Billy Franklin
City Brooks
Company Silvertip Outfitters
Contact Eric Grinnell
City Fort MacLeod
Company Skyline Trail Rides
Contact Dave Flato
City Jasper
Company Smith & Overguard Outfitting
Contact Jim Smith & Steve Overguard
City Sundre
Company South Paw Outfitters
Contact Rene & Kelly Semple
City Sangudo
Company South Ram Outfitters
Contact Lorne Hindbo
City Caroline
Company Sunset Guiding & Outfitting
Contact Duane D. Papke
City Sundre
Company Tall Timbers Outfitting
Contact David Sharp
City Bonnyville
Company Tom Scott Outfitting
Contact Tom Scott
City Westlock
Company Triple S Outfitting
Contact Stuart & Ruby Sinclair-Smith
City Calgary
Company Trophy Stalkers
Contact Doug Olson
City Edmonton
Company Tsayta Lake Lodge
Contact Graham Perry
City Rocky Mountain House
Company Vic Forchuk & Sons Outfitting & Guides
Contact Vic Forchuk
City Alder Flats
Company Warner Guiding & Outfitting
Contact Ron Warner
City Banff
Company Western Adventures
Contact Glenn & Leslie Huber
City Lathbridge
Company Western Guiding Services
Contact Dave & Greg Molloy
City Empress
Company Whispering Pine Outfitters
Contact Gordon & Lynn Utri
City Darwell
Company Wilderness Ranch
Contact Dick Hansen
City Claresholm
Company Willow Lane Ranch
Contact Keith & Leanne Lane
City Granum
Company Wind Valley Guiding & Outfitting
Contact Ken Fraser & Shelly Paul
City Cremona
Company Wolf-Creek Outfitters
Contact Robert Irvine
City Airdrie

British Columbia

Company 5 Star Wilderness
Contact
City Gold Bridge
Company A/Z Outfitters
Contact Bill DuBois
City Windermere
Company Albert Cooper Guide & Outfitters
Contact Albert Cooper
City Invermere
Company Alpine Ridge Guiding & Outfitting
Contact Allan Strauss
City Cranbrook
Company Andy Hagberg Guiding
Contact Andy Hagberg
City Prince George
Company Ashnola Guide & Outfitter
Contact Clarence Schneider
City Keremeos
Company Baldy Mountain Outfitters
Contact Harry Leuenberger
City Wardner
Company Bear Lake Guides & Outfitters
Contact Gerald Pattison
City Prince George
Company Blaine R. Southwick Outfitting
Contact Blaine Southwick
City Toad River
Company Bougie Mnt. Besa River Outfitting
Contact Paul Gillis
City Fort Nelson
Company Bowron River Guiding
Contact Jack Pichette
City North Vancouver
Company Bracewell's Alpine Wilderness Adventures
Contact Gerry Bracewell
City Tatlayolo Lake
Company Bradford & Co. Guide Services
Contact Myles & Sherry Bradford
City Dease Lake
Company Canadian Adventure Safaris
Contact Odd Aasland
City Cranbrook
Company Cariboo Mountain Outfitters
Contact Bradley Bowden
City Quesnel
Company Cariboo West Outfitters
Contact Gary & Peggy Zorn
City Williams Lake
Company Cassier Stone Outfitters
Contact Dan Stobbe
City Knutsford
Company Churn Creek Outfitters
Contact Eric Mikkelson
City Courtney
Company Coast Mountain Holidays
Contact Roma Richburg
City Tatla Lake
Company Collingwood Bros. Guides & Outfitters
Contact Ray & Reg Collingwood
City Smithers
Company Columbia River Outfitters
Contact Richard Hark
City Surrey
Company Copper River Ranch
Contact Ben Ridennoure
City Smithers
Company Coyote Creek
Contact Edward Cretney
City Fort Steele
Company Diamond M Outfitting
Contact Terry Spriggs
City Atlin

Company Double Eagle Guides & Outfitters
Contact Stewart Berg
City Granisle
Company Eagle Crest Guide Outfittters
Contact George Pedneault
City Sooke
Company East Kootenay Outfitters
Contact Joe Juozaitis
City Cranbrook
Company Echo Valley Ranch Resort
Contact
City Clinton
Company Finlay River Outfitters
Contact Rick McLean
City Prince George
Company Fournier Bros. Outfitting
Contact Greg Fournier
City Quesnel
Company Frontier Hunting
Contact Doug Davis
City Quesnel
Company G.F. Moore Enterprises
Contact Gordon F. Moore
City Dawson Creek
Company Gana River Outfitters
Contact Bill MacKenzie
City Quesnel
Company Granby Guides & Outfitters
Contact Barry Brandow
City Grand Forks
Company Grizzly Basin Outfitters
Contact Wilfrid Boardman
City Cranbrook
Company Grizzly Outfitters
Contact Phil Gillis
City Fort Nelson
Company Half Way Ranch Trail Rides
Contact
City Tatla Lake
Company Hallett Lake Outfitters
Contact Allen Ray
City Fort Fraser
Company Hodson Guiding Services
Contact D. Hodson
City Bella Coola
Company Icha & Illgatcho Mountain Outfitters
Contact Roger Williams
City Anahim Lake
Company Inzana Outfitters
Contact Terry Stocks
City Kamloops
Company Itcha Mountain Outfitters
Contact B.H. Fraser
City Quesnel
Company Kazchek Lake
Contact Harm Wernicke
City Langley
Company Kettle River Guides & Outfitters
Contact Melvin Kilback
City Oliver
Company Klukas Lake Ranch
Contact Glen Kilgour
City Taylor
Company Kyllo Brothers
Contact Scott Kyllo
City Hudson's Hope
Company Lamoureux Outfitters
Contact Martin Lamoureux
City Fort Ware
Company Layton Bryson Outfitting & Trail Riding
Contact Layton Bryson
City Lillooet
Company Lehman Creek Outfitters
Contact Dave Altherr
City Anahim Lake
Company Liard River Outfitters
Contact Mike Belfour
City Fort Nelson
Company M.C. Outfitting
Contact Chuck Christensen
City Edgewater
Company McCowan's Sporting Adventures
Contact Harry McCowan
City Kelowna
Company McKay Brothers Guides & Outfitters
Contact Bernard & Patrick McKay
City Prince George
Company Moose Valley Outfitters
Contact Ronald Steffey
City Germansen Landing
Company Mooseskin Johnny Lake Outfitters
Contact Don McIntyre
City Smithers
Company Muncho Lake Outfitters
Contact Arnold Henhapl
City Muncho Lake
Company Nahanni Butte Outfitters
Contact Greg Williams
City Charlie Lake
Company Nass Headwaters Guiding & Outfitting
Contact Ken Belford
City Smithers
Company Nisutlin Bay Outfitters
Contact Philip Smith
City Dawson Creek
Company North Coast Adventures
Contact Wayne Price
City Galiano
Company Norwest Guiding & Outfitting
Contact Jeff Beckley
City Cranbrook
Company Okanagan Outfitters
Contact Marc & Marcella Hubbard
City Penticton
Company Omineca Guide & Outfitters
Contact Herb Badey
City Prince George
Company Ottertail River Outfitting
Contact Alan & Mary Young
City Ft. St. John
Company Palliser River Guides & Outfitters
Contact Cody Tegart
City Radium
Company Parrot Mountain Outfitters
Contact Miles Fuller
City Burns Lake
Company Peace Country Wilderness Adventures
Contact Horst Mindermann
City Chetwynd
Company Peaceful Valley Wilderness Outfitters
Contact Len Pickering
City Prince George
Company Pine River Ventures
Contact Dale & Andy Copeland
City Montney
Company Pink Mountain Outfitters
Contact Klaur Knocke
City Burns Lake
Company Purcell Wilderness Guiding & Outfitting
Contact Gary E. Hansen
City Kimberley
Company Rainbow Mountain Outfitting
Contact David Dorsey
City Anahim Lake
Company Rocky Mountain Adventures
Contact Gordon Jeck
City McBride
Company Rocky Mountain High Outfitter & Guides
Contact Barry Scott
City Ft. Steele
Company Rocky Mountain Outfitters
Contact Carmen Dempsey
City Golden
Company Ross Peck Outfitters
Contact Ross Peck
City Ft. St. John
Company Sage Creek Outfitters
Contact Darrel Winser
City Elko
Company Salmon River Outfitters
Contact Dwayne Nikkels
City Lake Cowichan
Company Schuk Outfitting
Contact Doug Schuk
City Tatla Lake
Company Scoop Lake Outfittters
Contact Darwin Cary
City Kelowna
Company Sentinel Mountain Ent.
Contact Dave Drolet & Roy Pattison
City Bear Lake
Company Silent Mountain Outfitters
Contact Dieter Bohrmann
City Cranbrook
Company Smoke Mountain Guiding
Contact John Mould
City Burns Lake
Company Spruce Lake Outfitting
Contact Bryan Buchanan
City Sinclair Mills
Company Stein River Outfitters
Contact Leo & Doris Ouellet
City Hope
Company Stelkia Ranch
Contact Aaron Stelkia
City Oliver
Company Stone Mountain Safaris
Contact Dave & Ellie Wiens
City Toad River
Company Stuart-Trembleur Outfitters
Contact William Stanton

City Parksville
Company Sugar Valley Outfitters
Contact Bernie Jaeger
City Vernon
Company Suskeena Lodge
Contact Floyd Boyd
City Sorrento
Company Taku Safari
Contact Guy Anttila
City Atlin
Company Tatlatui Wilderness
Contact Bob Henderson
City Smithers
Company Three Bars Cattle & Guest Ranch
Contact Jeff & April Beckley
City Cranbrook
Company Toby Creek Outfitters
Contact Lloyd Harvey
City Cranbrook
Company Trophy West Guide Outfitters
Contact Donald Rose
City Campbell River
Company Ts'yl-os Park Lodge
Contact
City Williams Lake
Company Tukii Lodge
Contact Dave Hooper
City Smithers
Company Turnagain River Outfitters
Contact Eugene Egeler
City Kelowna
Company Uncha Mountain Outfitters
Contact Stefan Muehlmeyer
City Burns Lake
Company Vaseux Creek Outfitters
Contact Jim Wiens
City Oliver
Company Wayne Mueller Guide & Outfitters
Contact Wayne Mueller
City Sinclair Mills
Company Webb Outfitting
Contact Fred A. Webb
City Pritchard
Company Wolverine Mountain Outfitters
Contact Tim Chushman
City Wells

Labrador

Company Michikamau Outfitting
Contact
City Churchill Falls
Company True North Outfitting Co.
Contact Winston White
City Happy Valley - Goose Bay

Manitoba

Company Anderson's Outfitting Service
Contact Oscar Anderson
City South Indian Lake
Company Asmundson Outfitting Services
Contact Ed Asmundson
City Piney
Company Barta's Outfitting Service
Contact Stan Barta
City Hadashville
Company Bear Creek Outfitters
Contact Dieter Boehner
City Winnipeg
Company Big Antler Outfitters
Contact Ron Chekosky
City Poplarfield
Company Big Bear Outfitting
Contact Teddy Balcaen
City Petersfield
Company Big Game Outfitter
Contact John Reimer
City Grunthal
Company Birch Point Outfitters
Contact Erik Thienpondt
City Winnipeg
Company Bissett Outfitters
Contact Byron Grapentine
City Bissett
Company Blind Creek Outfitters
Contact Walter & Diane Dmyterko
City Fisher Branch
Company Bob's Wild West Adventures
Contact Bob Frost
City Elm Creek
Company Circle L Ranch
Contact Norm & Margo Leneal
City Stephenfield
Company D. W. Outfitting
Contact Daryl R. Woodbeck
City Beausejour
Company Darrell's Outfitting
Contact Darrell Dushanek
City The Pas
Company Dawson Bay Outfitters
Contact Ken Klyne
City Barrows
Company Desjardins Outfitter
Contact Alexis J. Desjardins
City Laurier
Company E & D Outfitters
Contact Ed Balan
City Olha
Company Fox River Outfitters
Contact Randy Naismith
City Gillam
Company Grandview Outfitting
Contact Thomas Ainsworth
City Grandview
Company Hazel Creek Outfitters
Contact Kurt Witt
City Hadashville
Company Head Water Ranch
Contact Bill McLeod
City Vassar
Company High Mountain Outfitters
Contact Dean Sandulak
City Kelwood
Company Hillbilly Outfitters
Contact Keith Tucker
City Mafeking
Company Johnson Road Outfitters
Contact Jim Wilson
City Thompson
Company K. C.'s Outfitting
Contact Ken C. Holme
City Grunthal
Company Lamaga's Guiding & Outfitting
Contact Myron Lamaga
City Hadashville
Company Manitoba North Outfitters
Contact Mel Podaima
City Fisher Branch
Company Manitoba Outfitters
Contact Tim Hastings & Dave Malko
City Bissett
Company Michie's Ranch & Lodge Outfitting
Contact David Michie
City Eriksdale
Company Northern Bear Adventure
Contact William Bruce Simms
City Thompson
Company Opaskwayak Guiding & Outfitting
Contact Thomas Cook & Chris Constant
City The Pas
Company Parkside Outfitting Service
Contact Boris Chuey
City Ethelbert
Company Pioneer Outfitters
Contact David or Charlene Doan
City Riding Montain
Company Pistol Lake Outfitters
Contact Joseph Cormier
City Flin Flon
Company Porcupine Mountain Outfitters
Contact Ed Racine
City Bellsite
Company Riding Mountain Guest Ranch
Contact Jim & Candy Irwin
City Audy Lake
Company Serene Lake Outfitters
Contact Ingi & Cindy Bjornson
City Cranberry Portage
Company Seton Trails Guest Lodge
Contact De'Athe Family
City Carberry
Company Smi's Outfitters
Contact David Semeniuk
City Pine River
Company Spruce Grove Outfitting
Contact George Bullock
City Swan River
Company Stag Lake Outpost Camp
Contact Keith Ripplinger
City Leaf Rapids
Company T & J Outfitters
Contact J.R. Zilinsky
City Winnipeg
Company Terry Neely Outfitters
Contact Terry Neely
City Benito
Company Trailhead Ranch

Contact Anne Schuster
City Lake Audy
Company Wallace Outfitters
Contact Kevin Allen
City Dugald
Company Waterhen First Nations Outfitting
Contact Melferd Carcheway
City Skownan
Company Woodlands Outfitting
Contact Clement Saulnier
City Snow Lake

New Brunswick

Company Craig's Sporting Camps
Contact Dale & Brian Craig
City Woodstock
Company Dorrington Hill Outfitters
Contact Shaun & Joy Collicott
City Canterbury
Company Harrison's Long Lake Sporting Camps
Contact Steve & Vicki Harrison
City Plaster Rock
Company Miramichi Four Season Outfitters, Inc.
Contact Thomas J. MacLean
City Newcastle
Company Northern Lights Lodge
Contact Dan Henry
City Plaster Rock
Company O'Donnells Cottages on the Miramichi
Contact Valerie O'Donnell
City Doaktown
Company Rousselle's Camp
Contact Gilles Rousselle
City Tracadie-Sheila
Company Silver Maple Lodge
Contact Bernard M. Duffy
City Renous
Company Tamarack Lodge
Contact John S. Davidson
City Debec
Company Victor Hunting Camp
Contact Victor Copp
City Plaster Rock
Company White Birch Lodge
Contact Andy Boss & Volker Strasser
City Newcastle
Company White Pine Lodge
Contact Paul & Barb Leahey
City Florenceville

Newfoundland

Company Adies Lake Hunting Lodge
Contact Don & Rod Stowe
City Pasadena
Company Blue Mountain Outfitters
Contact Carol & Adrian Payne
City Cow Head
Company Brophy & Sons
Contact
City Daniel's Harbour
Company Burnt Pond Outfitters
Contact Daniel Ryan
City Doyles
Company Caribou Valley Outfitters
Contact Donald & Yvonne Bonia
City Pasadena
Company Deer Pond Camps Ltd.
Contact Gregory Lucas
City Stephenville Crossing
Company Downey's Cabins
Contact Raymond Downey
City Doyles
Company Hammond Outfitters
Contact Leo Hammond
City Doyles
Company Hilliard's Cabins
Contact John T. Hilliard
City Codroy
Company Hilliard's Hunting Lodge
Contact Clifford Hilliard
City Codroy
Company Ida Patey & Sons
Contact Eric & Ida Patey
City St. Barbe Dist.
Company Iron Bound Outfitters
Contact Derreck Payne
City Daniel's Harbour
Company Long Range Outfitters
Contact G.J. Pumphrey
City
Company Moosehead Lodge
Contact Reginald White
City Buchans Junction
Company Mountain Top Cabin
Contact Wilfred Ryan
City O'Regans
Company O'Quinn's Outfitters
Contact Vincent O'Quinn
City
Company Owl's Nest Lodge Inc.
Contact Ron Parsons
City St. Johns
Company Peddle's Outfitting Ltd.
Contact Joseph Peddle
City Corner Brook
Company Portland Creek Outfitters Ltd.
Contact Leonard Payne & Aster Caines
City Portland Creek
Company RiverRun Outfitting & Tours Ltd
Contact Horace Lane
City Lewisporte
Company Rocky Ridge Lodge
Contact Denis Taverner & Tony Tuck
City Shoal Harbour
Company Stag Hill Outfitters
Contact Sam Kettle
City Grand Bay East
Company Steel Montain Lodge
Contact Ben Alexander
City St. George's
Company Tri-T Camps
Contact Tony Kenndey
City Upper Stewiache
Company Twin Valley Outfitters
Contact Eric & Kathy Cranford
City Pasadena
Company Woodland Lodge Ltd.
Contact Kevin Decker
City Parsons Pond

Northwest Territories

Company Adventure Northwest
Contact Bill Tait
City Yellowknife
Company Arviat HTO
Contact President George Kuksuk
City Arviat
Company Baker Lake HTA
Contact
City Baker Lake
Company Cadieux's Caribou Pass Outfitters
Contact Don Cadieux
City Yellowknife
Company Coppermine HTA
Contact
City Kugluktuk (Coppermine)
Company Deh Cho Wilderness Tours
Contact Digaa Enterprises
City Fort Providence
Company Ekaluktutiak (HTA)
Contact
City Cambridge Bay
Company Gjoa Haven Tours
Contact Paul Iqualluq
City Gjoa Haven
Company Mayukalik HTA
Contact
City Kimmirut (Lake Harbour)
Company Paulatuk HTC
Contact
City Paulatuk
Company Qutsiktukmiut Outfitting
Contact President David Akeeagok
City Grise Fiord
Company Rabesca's Resources, Camp Ekwo
Contact Moise & Joyce Rabesca
City Rae
Company Taloyoak HTA
Contact
City Taloyoak
Company The "J" Group/Peterson's Point Lake Camp
Contact The Petersons
City Yellowknife
Company Ulukhaktomiut HTC
Contact
City Holman
Company Umingmaktok HTA
Contact Jack Kaniak
City Umingmaktok (Baychimo)

Ontario

Company Air Ivanhoe Ltd.
Contact George & Jeanne Theriault
City Foleyet
Company Camp Des Grands Bois
Contact
City Bancrost
Company Camp Hiawatha
Contact Lloyd Lindner
City Birch Island
Company Camp Memewin
Contact
City Guelph
Company Camp Michi-Wawa
Contact Ken & Luanne Brezenski
City Wawa
Company Camp Sag-A-Me-Sing
Contact Davide & Barbara Weber
City Port Loring
Company Canada North Outfitting, Inc.
Contact
City Almonte
Company Chalet St-Hubert Enr.
Contact
City Brantfort
Company Chalets Du Huard/Chalets Scarf
Contact Ron & Mary Waye
City Powassan
Company Delay River Outfitters
Contact Craig Bogie
City Ottawa
Company Docks Inn Resort
Contact The Warkentins
City Mattawa
Company Gurney-By-The-Sea
Contact Roger & Linda Ferguson
City Terrace Bay
Company Hackl's Kashabowie River Resort
Contact Joe & Pat Hackl
City Shebandowan
Company Hart's Pine Falls Lodge
Contact The Harts
City Markstay
Company Ivanhoe Resort
Contact Russell & Shirley Litt
City Foleyet
Company James Bay Adventures
Contact Arthur Taillon
City Ottawa
Company Kenogaming Lodge
Contact Karen Radlowsky
City St. Catharines
Company Matabitchual Lodge
Contact Dieter & Marlis Maurer
City Temagami
Company Pavillon Du Lac Ogascanan Enr.
Contact
City North Bay
Company Pourvoirie Pommeroy Inc.
Contact
City Windsor
Company Pourvoirie Rodfam Inc.
Contact
City Windsor
Company Pourvoyeurs De La Riviere Delay Inc.
Contact
City Ottawa
Company Pourvoyeurs De La Riviere Ottawa Inc.
Contact
City Pembroke
Company Redden's Camp Ltd.
Contact Lorne & Pat Redden
City Longbow lake
Company Territoire De L'Orignal
Contact
City Pontiac Rolphton
Company Totomenai Lodge
Contact Frank & Susan Charbonneau
City Wawa
Company Woods Whiskey-Jack Lodge
Contact Terry & Lorna Wood
City Dryden

Prince Edward Island

Company Birch Grove Outfitters
Contact
City

Québec

Company George River Lodge
Contact Pierre Paquet
City Cap Rouge
Company Jack Hume Adventures Inc.
Contact Jack Hume
City Lachute
Company Moosehead Lodge
Contact Malcolm Taggart
City Messines

Saskatchewan

Company A & E Outfitters
Contact
City Biggar
Company A.R.M. Outfitters
Contact
City Shellbrook
Company All-Terrain Outfitters
Contact Marlon Parasiuk
City Stenen
Company All-The-Way-Holloway Outfitters
Contact
City Arcola
Company Barrier Chaparral Lodge
Contact George & Kasandra O'Bertos
City Tisdale
Company Bear Claw Outfitters
Contact
City Estevan
Company Bear Creek Outfitters
Contact
City Hudson Bay
Company Big Island Cove Resort
Contact
City Goodsoil
Company Big Sandy Resort
Contact Calvin & Annie Wingert
City Prince Albert
Company Bronson Lake Outfitters
Contact
City Battleford
Company Carrot Lake Outfitters
Contact
City Pierceland
Company Charlie Brown's Outfitting & Guiding Service
Contact
City Hazenmore
Company Circle Lakes Angus
Contact
City Mistatim
Company Clarke Lake Lodge/Clearwater Adv.
Contact
City Big River
Company Country Flavor
Contact Don & Linda Kirby
City Coronach
Company Cracking River Guides
Contact Al Fiddler
City Carrot River
Company Cree River Lodge
Contact
City Naicam
Company CutArm Outfitters
Contact
City Norquay
Company Dahl Creek Outfitting
Contact
City Hudson Bay
Company Deception Lake Lodge
Contact
City Fairy Glen
Company Delaronde Resort
Contact
City Big River
Company Dore Lake Lodge
Contact Alex & Vicky Shukin
City Big River
Company Eastview Wilderness Ranch
Contact Corrina Gray & Larry Kapeller
City Arborfield
Company Forsyth Ranch
Contact Ian & Irene Forsyth
City Tompkins
Company G W Outfitting
Contact Garry Walters
City Endeavour
Company Gary Simon Outfitting/ Thunder Rapids Lodge
Contact
City Carrot River
Company Ghost Ranch Outfitting
Contact Paul Chartrand
City St. Walburg
Company Greenwater & Marean Lake

Outfitting
Contact
City Archerwill
Company Hawks Point Pioneer Getaway
Contact Don & Elaine Nielsen
City Parry
Company John Fonos Outfitting
Contact
City Big River
Company K Bar T Vacation Ranch
Contact Keith & Eleanor Taylor
City Beechy
Company Kee Kamps Ltd.
Contact Dean Orosz or Barry Elton
City Saskatoon
Company Kelan Suffold Vacation Farm
Contact Ken & Lana Webster
City Elbow
Company Kutawag Lake Outfitter
Contact
City Semans
Company Lamplighter Lodge
Contact Roy & Cynthia Petrowicz
City Sturgis
Company Lone Spruce Outfitters
Contact Steven & Nancy Butler
City Loon Lake
Company Longview Farm
Contact Bob & Charlene Siemens
City Fiske
Company M & M Outfitters
Contact Moe Morley
City Chitek Lake
Company Magee's Farm
Contact Beatrice & Tom Magee
City Gull Lake
Company Martineau River Outfitters
Contact
City Pierceland
Company Medinski's Outfitting Services
Contact Larry Medynski
City Prince Albert
Company Minor Bay Camps
Contact Gerald & Paulette Howard
City Minton
Company Mistatim Outfitting
Contact
City Tisdale
Company Moen's Riverside Lodge
Contact
City Lacadena
Company Norseman Outfitters
Contact D. Rutherford & A. Kjerstad
City Birch Hills
Company Otter Basin Outfitters
Contact Don & Beverly Gillespie
City Mankota
Company Pickerel Point General Store
Contact Cliff & Susan Maruk
City Saskatoon
Company Pipe Stone Guiding
Contact
City Melfort
Company Pleasant Vista Farm
Contact George & Doris Husband
City Wawota
Company Prairieland Outfitters
Contact Don Anderson
City Rosetown
Company R P Outfitters
Contact
City Duck Lake
Company Rabbit Creek Outfitters
Contact Allan Folden
City Shellbrook
Company Riel Bosse Outfitting & Guiding
Contact
City Kelvington
Company Riverside Service & Cabins
Contact Ron Anderson
City Green Lake
Company Schmidt's Outdoor Expeditions
Contact
City Porcupine Plain
Company Schwab Simmentals
Contact David & Janet Schwab
City Big Beaver
Company Scott Lake Lodge
Contact Ken & Suzanne Gangler
City Stony Rapids
Company Skull Lodge
Contact
City Norquay
Company Spring Valley Guest Ranch
Contact Jim Saville
City Ravenscrag
Company Springwater Outfitters
Contact
City Cabri
Company Spruceville Outfitters
Contact Brian Washburn
City Hudson Bay
Company Squaw Creek Outfitters
Contact
City Loon Lake
Company The Stopping Place
Contact Deb & Ian McLeod & Family
City Ruthilda
Company Thunderhill Outfitter
Contact
City Saskatoon
Company Tower Lodge
Contact
City Saskatoon
Company W J Wilderness Camp
Contact James Custer
City Denare Beach
Company Wagons Roll Inn
Contact Lorraine & Ray Ostrom
City Diggar
Company Whiskey Jack Camp
Contact
City Ile a la Crosse
Company White Gull River Outfitters
Contact Tom McLane
City White Fox
Company Windy Acres Vacation Farm
Contact Elliot & Reta Kimpton
City Saskatoon
Company Wounded Knee
Contact Dick & Judy Wells
City Gull Lake
Company Wright's Vacation Farm
Contact Ken & Linda Wright
City Piapot

Yukon Territories

Company Arctic Red River Outfitters, Ltd.
Contact Kelly & Heather Hougen
City Whitehorse
Company Babala Stone Sheep Outfitters Ltd.
Contact Jim Babala
City Whitehorse
Company Blackstone Safaris
Contact Lee Bolster
City Whitehorse
Company Bonnet Plume Outfitters, Ltd.
Contact Charlie Stricker
City Whitehorse
Company Cassiar Mountain Outfitters
Contact Kirby Funnell
City Watson Lake
Company David Young Outfitters Ltd
Contact
City Whitehorse
Company Devilhole Outfitters
Contact
City Whitehorse
Company Dickson Outfitters Ltd.
Contact David Dickson
City Whitehorse
Company Heart Bar Ranch
Contact
City Whitehorse
Company Kluane Outfitters Ltd.
Contact Ross Elliott
City Whitehorse
Company Koser Outfitters
Contact Pete Koser
City Ross River
Company Kusawa Outfitters
Contact Klaas Heynen
City Whitehorse
Company MacMillan River Outfitters
Contact Dave Coleman
City Whitehorse
Company Nahanni-NWT Safaris
Contact Rick Furniss
City Whitehorse
Company Peter Jensen Guide & Outfitter
Contact Pete Jensen
City Whitehorse
Company Rainy Hollow Wilderness Adventures Ltd.
Contact
City Haines Junction
Company Rogue River Outfitters
Contact Cliff Hanna
City Whitehorse
Company Ruby Range
Contact Keith & Debbie Carreau
City Faro
Company Stan Reynolds Outfitting, Ltd.
Contact Stan Reynolds
City Dawson City

Company Sunshine Valley Guest Ranch
Contact
City Whitehorse
Company Teslin Outfitters
Contact Terry Wilkinson
City Watson Lake
Company Teslin Outfitters
Contact Doug Smarch
City Teslin
Company The Hitching Post
Contact
City Whitehorse
Company Wind River Wilderness Tours
Contact
City Mayo
Company Yukon Hunting & Guiding Ltd.
Contact Rod Hardie
City Whitehorse
Company Yukon Outfitting
Contact
City Whitehorse

Peel off your address label and place here

PLEASE NOTE: The Business or Professional you are invited to rate is printed above your name after "referred by..."

Top Rated Questionnaire
Western Adventures

Name of the Ranch:____________________________________

Name of your Host____________________ Length of your Stay____________

Date of Trip______________ Location____________________

Day Ride ☐ Pack Trip ☐ Cattle Drive ☐ Guest Ranch ☐ Other________

Was this a Family Trip where your children were actively involved in the activities? Yes ☐ No ☐

	Question	Outstanding	Excellent	Good	Acceptable	Poor/Inferior	Unacceptable
1.	How helpful was the Outfitter (Ranch or Pack Station) with travel arrangements, dates, special accommodations, etc.?	☐	☐	☐	☐	☐	☐
2.	How well did the Outfitter (Ranch or Pack Station) provide important details that better prepared you for your experience (clothing, list of "take along", etc.)?	☐	☐	☐	☐	☐	☐
3.	How would you rate the Outfitter's (Ranch or Pack Station) office skills in handling deposits, charges, reservations, returning calls before and after your trip?	☐	☐	☐	☐	☐	☐
4.	How would you rate the accommodations (bunk house, tent, cabin, lodge, etc.)?	☐	☐	☐	☐	☐	☐
5.	How would you rate the equipment provided by the Outfitter (Ranch or Pack Station) (horses, saddles, wagons, pick-ups, etc.)?	☐	☐	☐	☐	☐	☐
6.	How would you rate the cooking (quantity, quality and cleanliness of the service)?	☐	☐	☐	☐	☐	☐
7.	How would you rate your Guide/Host's attitude	☐	☐	☐	☐	☐	☐
8.	How would you rate your Guide/Host's professionalism?	☐	☐	☐	☐	☐	☐
9.	How would you rate your Guide/Host's disposition?	☐	☐	☐	☐	☐	☐
10.	How would you rate your Guide/Host's knowledge of the area?	☐	☐	☐	☐	☐	☐

	Outstanding	Excellent	Good	Acceptable	Poor/Inferior	Unacceptable
11. How would you rate your Guide/Host's knowledge of the livestock?...........	☐	☐	☐	☐	☐	☐
12. How would you rate your Guide/Host's handling of the livestock?..............	☐	☐	☐	☐	☐	☐
13. How would you rate the quality of the different activities offered during your stay (roping, branding, horse care, ranch life, etc.)?................................	☐	☐	☐	☐	☐	☐
14. How flexible was your Guide or Host in trying to meet your goal(s)?...........	☐	☐	☐	☐	☐	☐
15. How would you rate the overall quality of your outdoor experience?..........	☐	☐	☐	☐	☐	☐

	Good	Fair	Poor
16. How would you describe the weather conditions?..	☐	☐	☐

17. Was the overall quality of your experience (quality of animals, activities, and accommodations, etc.) accurately represented by the Outfitter (Ranch or Pack Station)? .... ☐ Yes ☐ No

18. Did you provide the Outfitter (Ranch or Pack Station) with truthful statements regarding your personal needs, your skills and your expectations?.. ☐ Yes ☐ No

19. Would you use this Outdoor Professional/Business again?........................... ☐ Yes ☐ No

20. Would you recommend this Outdoor Professional/Business to others?..... ☐ Yes ☐ No

Comments: ____

____

____

____

____

____

____

____

____

____

____

____

____

____

____

____

____

____

____

____

Will you permit Picked-By-You to use your name and comments in our book(s)? ☐ Yes ☐ No

Signature____________________________

Photo Credits

Double Spear Ranch/©Sorrel 83
Nine Quarter Circle Ranch/©Dann Coffey 97

Ranches, Outfitters and Pack Stations by Activity

Archery

Coffee Creek Ranch
Cornucopia Wilderness Pack Stn.
Esper's Under Wild Skies
EW Watson & Sons
Echo Canyon Ranch
Granite Creek Guest Ranch
Iron Wheel Ranch
Maynard Ranch
Outback Ranch Outfitters
Spanish Spring Ranch

Barrel Racing

Clear Creek Ranch
Coffee Creek Ranch
Early Guest Ranch
Hidden Hollow Hideway
Spanish Spring Ranch
Trailhead Ranch

Big Game Hunting

Beartooth Plateau Outfitters
Boulder Lake Lodge
Cheff Guest Ranch
Coffee Creek Ranch
Cornucopia Wilderness Pack Stn.
Darby Mountain Outfitters
Darwin Ranch
Echo Canyon
Esper's Under Wild Skies
EW Watson & Sons
Frazier Outfitting
K Bar Z Guest Ranch
Hidden Hollow Hideway
Iron Wheel Ranch
John Henry Lee Outfitters
Lakeview Resort
Lost Creek Ranch
Lozier's Box "R" Ranch
Monture Face Outfitters
Outback Ranch Outfitters
Paintrock Adventures
San Juan Outfitting
Steens Mountain Packers
Triangle C Ranch
WTR Outfittters
Wind River Outfitters

Branding

Cheff Guest Ranch
Double Spear Ranch
Early Guest Ranch
Echo Canyon Ranch
EW Watson & Sons
Hargrave Cattle & Guest Ranch
Hartley Guest Ranch
Hidden Hollow Hideway
Lozier's Box "R" Ranch
Maynard Ranch
Outback Ranch Outfitters
Spanish Spring Ranch
Three Cross Ranch

Ranches, Outfitters and Pack Stations by Activity

Cattle and Horse Drives

Cheff Guest Ranch
Double Spear Ranch
Echo Canyon Ranch
EW Watson & Sons
Granite Creek Guest Ranch
Hargrave Cattle & Guest Ranch
Hartley Guest Ranch
Hidden Hollow Hideway
Little Knife Outfitters
Lozier's Box "R" Ranch
Maynard Ranch
Outback Ranch Outfitters
Steen Mountain Packers
Three Cross Ranch

Children/Youth

Beartooth Plateau Outfitters
Clear Creek Ranch
Coffee Creek Ranch
Granite Creek Guest Ranch
Iron Wheel Ranch
Maynard Ranch
Nine Quarter Circle Ranch
Rich Ranch
Skyline Guest Ranch
Three Cross Ranch
Triangle C Ranch
Venture Outdoors

Cowboy and Live Entertainment

Coffee Creek Ranch
Early Guest Ranch
Echo Canyon Guest Ranch
Granite Creek Guest Ranch
Hargrave Cattle & Guest Ranch
Maynard Ranch
Schmittel Packing and Outfitting
Skyline Guest Ranch
Triangle C Ranch

Clay Shooting

Echo Canyon Ranch
Hargrave Cattle & Guest Ranch
Spanish Spring Ranch

Cross Country Skiing

Beaver Meadows Resort Ranch
Coffee Creek Ranch
Cornucopia Wilderness Pack Stn.
Darwin Ranch
Hargrave Cattle & Guest Ranch
K Bar Z Guest Ranch
Rich Ranch
Skyline Guest Ranch
Spanish Spring Ranch

Cutting

Granite Creek Guest Ranch
Hargrave Cattle & Guest Ranch
Lozier's Box "R" Ranch

Ranches, Outfitters and Pack Stations by Activity

Dancing

Clear Creek Ranch
Early Guest Ranch
Nine Quarter Circle Ranch
Spanish Spring Ranch
Triangle C Ranch

Fishing

Cheff Guest Ranch
Clear Creek Ranch
Darby Mountain Outfitters
Early Guest Ranch
Echo Canyon Ranch
Esper's Under Wild Skies
Frazier Outfitting
Granite Creek Guest Ranch
Hartley Guest Ranch
Iron Wheel Ranch
K Bar Z Guest Ranch
Lakeview Resort
Maynard Ranch
Nine Quarter Circle Ranch
Outback Ranch Outfitters
San Juan Outfitting
Schmittel Packing and Outfitting
Skyline Guest Ranch
Spanish Spring Ranch
Trailhead Ranch
Wallowa Llamas
WTR Outfitters

Fly Fishing

Absaroka Ranch
Beartooth Plateau Outfitters
Beaver Meadows Resort Ranch
Boulder Lake Lodge
Broken Arrow Lodge
Cheff Guest Ranch
Clear Creek Ranch
Coffee Creek Ranch
Cornucopia Wilderness Pack Stn.
Darby Mountain Outfitters
Darwin Ranch
Double Spear Ranch
Early Guest Ranch
Echo Canyon Ranch
Esper's Under Wild Skies
EW Watson & Sons
Frazier Outfitting
Hargrave Cattle & Guest Ranch
Hidden Hollow Hideway
Iron Wheel Ranch
K Bar Z Guest Ranch
Lakeview Resort
Lost Creek Ranch
Lozier's Box "R" Ranch
Maynard Ranch
Monture Face Outfitters
Nine Quarter Circle Ranch
Paintrock Adventures
Rich Ranch
San Juan Outfitting
Skyline Guest Ranch
Steens Mountain Packers
Trailhead Ranch
Triangle C Ranch
Wallowa Llamas
WTR Outfitters

Float Fishing

Darby Mountain Outfitters

Ranches, Outfitters and Pack Stations by Activity

Golfing

Clear Creek Ranch
Echo Canyon Ranch
Trailhead Ranch
Skyline Guest Ranch

Ghost Town Tours

Early Guest Ranch
EW Watson & Sons
Iron Wheel Ranch
Skyline Guest Ranch
Venture Outdoors

Hiking/Trekking Excursions

Absaroka Ranch
Broken Arrow Lodge
Cheff Guest Ranch
Clear Creek Ranch
Cornucopia Wilderness Pack Stn.
Darby Mountain Outfitters
Darwin Ranch
Early Guest Ranch
Esper's Under Wild Skies
Frazier Outfitting
Granite Creek Guest Ranch
Hartley Guest Ranch
K Bar Z Guest Ranch
Lost Creek Ranch
Lozier's Box "R" Ranch
Maynard Ranch
Nine Quarter Circle Ranch
Outback Ranch Outfitters
Paintrock Adventures
S.A.L.E.M. Treks
Skyline Guest Ranch
Spanish Spring Ranch
Steens Mountain Packers
Three Cross Ranch
Trailhead Ranch
Triangle C Ranch
Venture Outdoors
Wallowa Llamas
WTR Outfitters

Horseback Riding

Absaroka Ranch
Beartooth Plateau Outfitters
Beaver Meadows Resort Ranch
Boulder Lake Lodge
Broken Arrow Lodge
Cheff Guest Ranch
Clear Creek Ranch
Coffee Creek Ranch
Cornucopia Wilderness Pack Stn.
Darby Mountain Outfitters
Darwin Ranch
Double Spear Ranch
Early Guest Ranch
Echo Canyon Ranch
Esper's Under Wild Skies
EW Watson & Sons
Frazier Outfitting
Granite Creek Guest Ranch
Hargrave Cattle & Guest Ranch
Hartley Guest Ranch
Hidden Hollow Hideway
Iron Wheel Ranch
John Henry Lee Outfitters
K Bar Z Guest Ranch
Lakeview Resort
Little Knife Outfitters
Lost Creek Ranch
Lozier's Box "R" Ranch
Maynard Ranch
Monture Face Outfitters
Nine Quarter Circle Ranch
Paintrock Adventures
Rich Ranch
San Juan Outfitting
Schmittel Packing and Outfitting

Ranches, Outfitters and Pack Stations by Activity

Skyline Guest Ranch
Spanish Spring Ranch
Steens Mountain Packers
Three Cross Ranch
Trailhead Ranch
Triangle C Ranch
WTR Outfitters
Wind River Outfitters

Horse Pack Trips

Absaroka Ranch
Beartooth Plateau Outfitters
Boulder Lake Lodge
Broken Arrow Lodge
Cheff Guest Ranch
Cornucopia Wilderness Pack Stn.
Darby Mountain Outfitters
Darwin Ranch
Double Spear Ranch
Early Guest Ranch
Echo Canyon Ranch
Esper's Under Wild Skies
EW Watson & Sons
Frazier Outfitting
Hargrave Cattle & Guest Ranch
Hartley Guest Ranch
Hidden Hollow Hideway
John Henry Lee Outfitters
K Bar Z Guest Ranch
Lakeview Resort
Little Knife Outfitters
Lost Creek Ranch
Lozier's Box "R" Ranch
Maynard Ranch
Monture Face Outfitters
Nine Quarter Circle Ranch
Paintrock Adventure
Rich Ranch
San Juan Outfitting
Schmittel Packing and Outfitting
Skyline Guest Ranch
Steens Mountain Packers
Three Cross Ranch
Trailhead Ranch
Triangle C Ranch
WTR Outfitters
Wind River Outfitters

Cowboy Games

Beaver Meadows Resort Ranch
Boulder Lake Lodge
Broken Arrow Lodge
Cheff Guest Ranch
Coffee Creek Ranch
Darby Mountain Outfitters
Early Guest Ranch
Echo Canyon Ranch
Granite Creek Guest Ranch
Hargrave Cattle & Guest Ranch
Hidden Hollow Hideway
Iron Wheel Ranch
John Henry Lee Outfitters
K Bar Z Guest Ranch
Lozier's Box "R" Ranch
Maynard Ranch
Nine Quarter Circle Ranch
Outback Ranch Outfitters
Three Cross Ranch
Triangle C Ranch

Llama Pack Trips

S.A.L.E.M. Treks
Venture Outdoors
Wallowa Llamas

Mountain Biking

Beaver Meadows Resort Ranch
Echo Canyon Ranch
Skyline Guest Ranch
Steens Mountain Packers
Trailhead Ranch
Venture Outdoors

Ranches, Outfitters and Pack Stations by Activity

Raft / Float Trips

Clear Creek Ranch
Cornucopia Wilderness Pack Stn.
Early Guest Ranch
Echo Canyon Ranch
EW Watson & Sons
Hargrave Cattle & Guest Ranch
Hartley Guest Ranch
Iron Wheel Ranch

Roping

Clear Creek Ranch
Double Spear Ranch
Echo Canyon Ranch
EW Watson & Sons
Granite Creek Guest Ranch
Hargrave Cattle & Guest Ranch
Hidden Hollow Hideway
Lozier's Box "R" Ranch
Trailhead Ranch

School, Fly Fishing

Skyline Guest Ranch

School, Riding

Beaver Meadows Resort Ranch
Broken Arrow Lodge
Cheff Guest Ranch
Darby Mountain Outfitters
Double Spear Ranch
Early Guest Ranch
Echo Canyon Ranch
Hargrave Cattle & Guest Ranch
Iron Wheel Ranch
John Henry Lee Outfitters
Nine Quarter Circle Ranch
Skyline Guest Ranch
Spanish Spring Ranch
Steens Mountain Packers

School, Horse Packing

Boulder Lake Lodge
Iron Wheel Ranch
Hidden Hollow Hideway
Maynard Ranch
Paintrock Adventures
Steens Mountain Packers
Trailhead Ranch
Triangle C Ranch

School, Horse Shoeing

Iron Wheel Ranch

Ranches, Outfitters and Pack Stations by Activity

Snowshoeing

Beaver Meadows Resort Ranch
Coffee Creek Ranch
Skyline Guest Ranch
Steens Mountain Packers

Target Shooting

Broken Arrow Lodge
Coffee Creek Ranch
Double Spear Ranch
Echo Canyon Ranch
Esper's Under Wild Skies
EW Watson & Sons
Granite Creek Guest Ranch
Hargrave Cattle & Guest Ranch
Hidden Hollow Hideway
Iron Wheel Ranch
Lost Creek Ranch
Lozier's Box "R" Ranch
Maynard Ranch
Spanish Spring Ranch

Team Penning

Granite Creek Guest Ranch
Hargrave Cattle & Guest Ranch

Team Roping

Early Guest Ranch

Wagon Rides

Beaver Meadows Resort Ranch
Coffee Creek Ranch
Cornucopia Wilderness Pack Stn.
Echo Canyon Ranch
EW Watson & Sons
Lozier's Box "R" Ranch
Maynard Ranch
Nine Quarter Circle Ranch
Spanish Spring Ranch
Three Cross Ranch
Trailhead Ranch
Triangle C Ranch

Wildlife Viewing

Absaroka Ranch
Beartooth Plateau Outfitters
Broken Arrow Lodge
Darby Mountain Outfitters
Darwin Ranch
Frazier Outfitting
Hidden Hollow Hideway
John Henry Lee Outfitters
K Bar Z Guest Ranch
Little Knife Outfitters
Lozier's Box "R" Ranch
Monture Face Outfitters
Nine Quarter Circle Ranch
Paintrock Adventures
San Juan Outfitting
Schmittel Packing and Outfitting
Steens Mountain Packers
Three Cross Ranch
Triangle C Ranch
Venture Outdoors

Ranches, Outfitters and Pack Stations by State

Ranches, Outfitters and Pack Stations by State/Province

Alphabetical Index by Company Name